THE ULTIMATE BOOK OF AMAZING ANIMAL FACTS

MORE THAN 1600 INCREDIBLE, FASCINATING AND ENTERTAINING BITS OF INFORMATION ABOUT THE WILDLIFE OF THE WORLD

THE INTERNET CROW

Find more fascinating books and facts at **www.theinternetcrow.com**.

CONTENTS

ALLIGATORS AND CROCODILES

ALLIGATORS AND CROCODILES are some of the most fascinating creatures in the animal kingdom. Both species have unique physical features, behaviors, and adaptations that make them incredibly successful predators and survivors. Here are some amazing facts about alligators and crocodiles:

- Alligators have an impressive bite force of 2,125 psi.
- Crocodiles can hold their breath underwater for up to two hours.
- Alligators can swim up to 20 miles per hour.
- Crocodiles can go through up to 3,000 teeth in their lifetime.
- Alligators have a sensory organ in the roof of their mouths which helps them detect vibrations in the water.
- Crocodiles can survive in saltwater and freshwater.
- Alligators can live up to 50 years in the wild.
- Crocodiles can go days without eating.
- Alligators have four short, webbed toes on their hind feet.

- Crocodiles can "sneeze" out water to expel debris from their noses.
- Alligators have powerful tails that can propel them through the water at high speeds.
- Crocodiles can regulate their internal temperature by opening and closing their mouths.
- Alligators are able to raise their heads above water while their bodies remain submerged.
- Crocodiles can move on land at speeds up to 17 miles per hour.
- Alligators can lay up to 50 eggs at a time.

ALPACAS AND LLAMAS

ALPACAS AND LLAMAS are fascinating animals native to the South American Andes. They both have long necks, slender bodies, and soft fur and can weigh up to 150 lbs. Alpacas are smaller than llamas, and their fur is used to make luxurious clothing and products. Amazing facts about Alpacas and Llamas:

- Alpacas and llamas are both members of the camelid family
- They have three-chambered stomachs to help them digest tough vegetation
- Alpacas come in 22 distinct colors
- An alpaca can live up to 20 years
- Llamas can carry up to 25% of their body weight
- Alpacas have padded feet which help prevent soil erosion
- Llamas have a unique vocalization which serves as a warning call
- Alpacas are highly social animals and live in herds
- Llamas can be taught to pull carts and be ridden

- Alpacas have an inner layer of fur which is highly insulating
- Llamas have excellent eyesight and hearing
- Alpacas have soft padded lips which help them pick up small food particles
- Llamas have a gestation period of 11 months
- Alpacas are shorn once a year
- Llamas produce a unique type of wool which is very strong and warm

ANTS

ANTS ARE some of the most fascinating creatures on earth. They are incredibly strong, efficient and highly intelligent, and able to lift over 50 times their own body weight and build complex underground colonies. Here are some amazing facts about ants:

- Ants have been on Earth for over 100 million years.
- Ants can be found on every continent except Antarctica.
- There are over 12,000 species of ants in total.
- Ants have a highly developed sense of smell and use it to communicate with each other.
- Ants can work together as a team to accomplish tasks up to 1000 times the weight of all the ants combined.
- Ants can run at speeds up to 300 body lengths per second.
- Ants have an accurate internal clock that helps them to know when to start and stop foraging for food.

- Ants use their antennae to touch, taste and smell their environment and communicate with each other chemically.
- Ants have strong jaws and can bite with a force of up to 1,000 lbs per square inch.
- Ants can survive up to 7 weeks without food or water.
- Ants are social and live in colonies with up to 500,000 members.
- Ants can recognize the chemical scent of their nest mates and can distinguish between the two major castes of workers and queens.
- Ants have the ability to learn complex behaviours.
- Ants can move their nests to adapt to changing environment conditions.
- Ants can live up to 30 years.

ANTEATERS

ANTEATERS ARE amazing animals that have evolved a wide range of adaptations for living in their distinct habitats. These amazing animals are known for their long snouts and sticky tongues, which they use to eat their favorite food: ants and termites. They also have powerful claws for digging, and a muscular body that helps them break into ant colonies.

- Anteaters have no teeth and rely on their long tongues to eat and get nourishment.
- Anteaters have a two-fingered forefoot and a two-toed hindfoot that allow them to grasp and hang onto branches while they feed.
- The tongues of an anteater can reach up to 60 cm in length, and they can move their tongue at an amazing speed of 150 times per minute.
- Anteaters have poor vision, but they make up for it with their highly advanced sense of smell.
- Anteaters can consume up to 35,000 ants in a single day.
- An adult anteater can weigh up to 20 kg, and can measure up to 1.5 metres in length.

- Anteaters have long claws which help them break open ant and termite colonies.
- Most species of anteaters are solitary animals, although some, such as the giant anteater, can form small groups of up to four individuals.
- Anteaters can live up to 15 years in the wild.
- Anteaters are native to Central and South America and can be found in a variety of habitats, including forests, grasslands, and even deserts.
- The giant anteater is the largest species of anteater and can reach up to 1.8 m in length.
- Anteaters are great swimmers, and some species are even capable of using their long tongues to fish for food in the water.
- Anteaters are great climbers and can use their long claws to climb up to the highest branches of trees.
- The front claws of an anteater are so sharp and powerful that they have been known to puncture a human's skin.
- Anteaters have a thick coat of fur that helps protect them from the elements and predators.

ANTELOPES AND DEER

ANTELOPES AND DEER are among the most majestic animals on the planet. Both species have adapted to survive in a wide range of climates and habitats, allowing them to exist in many different parts of the world. Moreover, they have several unique and fascinating characteristics. Here are some amazing facts about antelopes and deer:

- Antelopes and deer have hooves that are split into two sections, allowing them to move quickly and maneuver nimbly.
- Antelopes and deer can jump up to 3 metres in the air, making them one of the best jumpers in the animal kingdom.
- While most deer have antlers, only male antelopes are born with horns.
- Both antelopes and deer have a keen sense of smell, which helps them to detect predators.
- Male antelopes and deer use their horns and antlers to fight for dominance during mating season.
- Female antelopes and deer are able to give birth to up to 3 young per pregnancy.

- Antelopes and deer can run up to 50 kilometres per hour.
- Deer have the ability to move each of their ears independently, giving them a wide range of hearing capabilities.
- Antelopes and deer will often stand still or flee when a predator is present, as they cannot outrun most of them.
- Since antelopes and deer are herbivores, their diet consists of grasses, leaves, and fruits.
- Antelopes and deer have wide eyes that give them excellent peripheral vision.
- Antelopes and deer can live up to 10-20 years in the wild.
- Antelopes and deer are very social animals and often live in herds of up to 30 individuals.
- Antelopes and deer shed their horns every year, and regrow them in the spring.
- Antelopes and deer have a unique alarm call that helps alert other members of their herd when danger is present.

ARMADILLOS

ARMADILLOS ARE fascinating creatures that thrive in the warm climates of the Americas. Known for their protective armor, armadillos can move quickly, dig deep burrows, and jump up to three feet in the air! Here are some amazing facts about armadillos:

- Armadillos can be found in the southern United States, Central America, and South America.
- The average armadillo can live between 15 and 20 years in the wild.
- Armadillos are nocturnal animals, so they are mostly active at night.
- Armadillos have poor eyesight, but their sense of smell and hearing is very strong.
- Armadillos are omnivores, so they eat both plants and small animals.
- The armadillo's armor is made of a substance called keratin, which is the same material that makes up human hair and nails.
- Armadillos are solitary animals, meaning they do not live in groups.

- Armadillos can hold their breath underwater for up to 6 minutes.
- Armadillos are capable of rolling up into a tight ball to protect themselves from predators.
- Armadillos are excellent swimmers and can even remain submerged for up to 5 minutes at a time.
- Some species of armadillo can jump up to three feet in the air when startled.
- Armadillos can carry and spread the bacteria that cause leprosy.
- Some species of armadillos have the ability to walk on water.
- Armadillos can run at speeds of up to 25 miles per hour.
- Female armadillos usually give birth to four identical offspring at a time.

BADGERS

BADGERS ARE INCREDIBLY interesting and unique animals. They are the largest land-dwelling species of the Mustelidae family and are known for their particularly fierce and protective nature. Badgers are highly social creatures, living in clans of up to 15 individuals and are even known to help each other with digging and food gathering.

- Badgers belong to the Mustelidae family, which includes animals such as ferrets, otters, weasels, and wolverines.
- Badgers have been found to live up to 15 years in the wild.
- They are nocturnal animals, meaning they are most active at night.
- Badgers are omnivores, meaning they will eat both plants and animals.
- They have a particular fondness for bees and honey.
- Badgers live in complex burrows, known as setts, which can measure up to 30m in length.
- Badgers are incredibly strong and fast animals – they can run up to 30km/h.

- They have a thick, bristly coat made up of greyish-brown fur on the back and white fur on the throat and chest.
- Badgers have an incredibly strong sense of smell, which they use to help them find food.
- Badgers are highly social animals and form clans of up to 15 individuals.
- They are known to help each other in activities such as digging and food gathering.
- Badgers are particularly fierce and protective animals.
- They have long, sharp claws used for digging and defense.
- Badgers are excellent swimmers and can stay underwater for up to 5 minutes.
- Badgers are a keystone species and play an important role in the ecosystem.

BATS

BATS ARE INCREDIBLY UNIQUE CREATURES, with many remarkable qualities. They can fly up to sixty miles per hour, and have the ability to turn in mid-flight, adapting to their environment in incredible ways. They use echolocation to find their prey, and many species migrate to different habitats depending on the season. Here are some amazing facts about bats:

- Bats are the only mammals capable of true, sustained flight.
- The largest bat in the world is the giant golden-crowned flying fox, with a wingspan of up to 5.5 feet.
- Many species of bat live up to 30 years in the wild.
- Bats eat up to half their body weight in insects each night.
- Bats are the only mammal known to carry rabies less than one percent of the time.
- Some species of bat give birth to only one baby each year.

- Bats make up nearly a quarter of all mammals found on Earth.
- Bats are the only mammal to use sophisticated echolocation to find their prey and navigate.
- Bats are capable of flying at altitudes of up to 10,000 feet.
- There are over 1,200 species of bat worldwide.
- Bats are the only mammal with the ability to adapt to the changing of the seasons, migrating to different habitats depending on the climate.
- The smallest bat in the world, the bumblebee bat, is only about the size of a thumbnail.
- Bats are incredibly important to the environment, pollinating plants, dispersing seeds, and controlling pests like mosquitoes and crop-damaging insects.
- Bats can live up to 20 years in captivity.
- Some species of bats can hibernate for up to six months.

BEARS

SEE ALSO: POLAR BEARS, PANDAS

BEARS ARE FASCINATING CREATURES, with incredible adaptations to their environment. They have powerful senses of smell, sharp claws and teeth, thick fur for insulation, and are incredibly smart, with some species being able to recognize themselves in a mirror. Here are some amazing facts about them:

- Bears are found in a wide variety of habitats, from the Arctic to warm, temperate forests.
- The smallest bear species, the sun bear, is just 1.2 meters long and weighs only 35 kilograms.
- Bears can run at speeds of up to 40 miles per hour.
- Bears can swim up to 6 miles per hour.
- Bears use their sense of smell to find food and identify other bears.
- Some bears hibernate for up to 8 months of the year.
- Some species of bears have been known to live for over 30 years in the wild.
- Bears can stand on their hind legs for extended periods of time.

- Bears are omnivores and will eat both plants and animals.
- Black bears can climb trees.
- Grizzlies have the strongest bite of any land mammal.
- Sloth bears have a temperature-regulating tongue that helps them digest honey.
- Sun bears have long tongues they use to eat ants and termites.

BEAVERS

BEAVERS ARE AMAZING ANIMALS, renowned for their hardworking nature and remarkable engineering skill. From building dams to creating ponds, their industriousness and resourcefulness is unparalleled. Here are some amazing facts about beavers:

- Beavers have orange-tinted fur, which helps them camouflage in and around their natural habitats.
- Beavers are the largest rodent in North America, reaching up to 4 feet in length and weighing up to 60 pounds.
- Beavers have strong, chisel-like front teeth that never stop growing and allow them to easily cut through trees.
- Beavers build dams to slow down the flow of water, creating deep ponds that are home to many other animals.
- Beavers are nocturnal, meaning they are most active at night and sleep during the day.

- Beavers have flaps of skin on their rumps that allow them to close their rear ends when they swim underwater.
- Beavers use mud, rocks, and sticks to construct their dams and lodges.
- Beavers often live up to 24 years in the wild.
- Beavers have a broad diet that includes grass, bark, leaves, stems, twigs, aquatic plants, and even fish.
- Beavers are capable of swimming up to 6 miles per hour.
- Beavers often communicate with each other through various sounds, including slapping their tails on the water.
- Beavers can secrete a special oil from their glands to waterproof their fur.
- Beavers have webbed feet that allow them to swim with better speed and agility.
- Beavers use their flat tails as a rudder to steer in the water.
- Beavers are essential to the ecology of their habitat, as they create wetlands that are home to many other animals.

BEES AND WASPS

BEES AND WASPS are some of the most fascinating insects in the world. They have amazing social behaviors, sophisticated communication methods and specialized body parts that enable them to navigate and thrive in their environment. Here are some amazing facts about bees and wasps:

- Bees and wasps have over 20,000 unique species worldwide.
- Bees have five eyes and three simple eyes, providing them with 360-degree vision.
- Bees have hair on their eyes that helps them detect air motion and vibrations.
- Bees have branched antennae that act like a nose and help them detect smells.
- Bees can see in the ultraviolet spectrum, allowing them to recognize different types of flowers.
- Wasps have smooth bodies, which are covered in scales that help protect them against predators.
- Wasps have two pairs of wings and some species are capable of flight speeds of up to 25 mph.

- Wasps can sting multiple times and create a venom that affects the victim's nervous system.
- Bees communicate with each other through a waggle dance that conveys information about the location of food sources.
- Bees can carry up to 70% of their body weight in pollen.
- Honeybees can fly up to 6 miles from the hive in search of food.
- Worker bees live for about 6 weeks during the summer and for up to 6 months during the winter.
- Wasps can be important predators of pests, such as aphids, caterpillars and flies.
- Wasps use mud to create their nests and can often be seen carrying mud in their jaws.
- Wasps create their nests from paper that is made from chewed wood and plant fibers.

BIG CATS

SEE ALSO: LIONS, TIGERS, CHEETAHS, JAGUARS

BIG CATS ARE some of the most majestic and awe-inspiring creatures on the planet. Other than lions and tigers, there are many other big cats that are equally as impressive. Here are some amazing facts about big cats other than lions and tigers:

- The puma, or cougar, is the most widespread big cat in the Americas.
- The snow leopard is able to leap up to 15 metres (49 feet) in a single bound.
- The leopard can carry prey weighing up to twice its own body weight up into tree branches to avoid other predators.
- The clouded leopard is the only big cat with the ability to purr, but not roar.
- The Eurasian lynx is the largest species of lynx, reaching up to 81 cm (32 in) at the shoulder.
- The caracal is able to jump up to 3 metres (10 feet) high to catch birds in mid-flight.
- The African golden cat is an incredibly rare species that is found only in the rainforests of Africa.

- The sunda clouded leopard is found only in the tropical forests of Southeast Asia.
- The Pallas's cat is one of the smallest big cats and is found in the high mountains of Central Asia.
- The bobcat is found from southern Canada to northern Mexico and is the most common species of wild cat in North America.
- The fishing cat is an aquatic species that is found in the wetlands of Southeast Asia.
- The black-footed cat is the smallest African cat and is found in the semi-deserts of southern Africa.
- The ocelot is found in the forests of South and Central America and is one of the most endangered species of wild cat.

BIRDS OF PREY

SEE ALSO: OWLS

BIRDS OF PREY, also known as raptors, are an amazing group of birds that possess a wide array of adaptations and features that make them unique. They have exceptional visual acuity and incredibly sharp talons which they use to capture and kill their prey. Their diet consists mainly of small animals with some species even preying on fish.

- Raptors can spot prey up to two miles away.
- Eagles have a wingspan of up to 8 feet wide.
- Raptors have powerful legs and talons which enable them to capture their prey.
- The peregrine falcon is the fastest bird in the world, reaching speeds of over 200 mph during a dive.
- Raptors have a powerful beak that helps them tear flesh and crush bones.
- Ospreys have reversible toes with two toes facing forward and two facing back which helps them hold onto slippery prey.
- Hawks, eagles, and owls all use different hunting strategies.

- Some species of raptors migrate long distances each year.
- Raptors can live up to 19 years in the wild.
- Falcons use their wings to generate lift as they dive for prey.
- Raptors have excellent eyesight which allows them to spot prey from great distances.
- Vultures have a bald head that helps them stay clean in their scavenging duties.
- Ospreys are the only raptor that specializes in catching fish.

BUFFALOES

BUFFALOES ARE amazing and fascinating animals. They are agile and strong, with some individuals possessing the ability to run up to 40 miles per hour. They are also incredibly intelligent, and have been known to remember paths, directions and locations up to three years later. They are an integral part of many local cultures, and are also known for their loyalty and strength.

- The American bison, commonly referred to as a buffalo, is the largest land mammal in North America.
- Buffaloes are herbivores and primarily feed on grasses, sedges, and other aquatic vegetation.
- The average lifespan of a buffalo is 15 to 20 years in the wild, while they can live up to 30 years in captivity.
- Buffaloes can reach a weight of up to 2,000kg (4,400lbs).
- Buffaloes are found in countries like India, South Africa and Australia.

- Buffaloes have a thick, shaggy coat that helps keep them warm in cold climates.
- Buffaloes are very social animals and live in herds.
- Buffaloes are able to swim and can stay submerged underwater for up to 5 minutes.
- Females usually give birth to a single calf every two years.
- Male buffaloes are called bulls, while female buffaloes are called cows.
- Buffaloes are able to identify other members of their herd by their vocalizations.
- Buffaloes are capable of detecting danger, and will alert their herd when danger is nearby.
- The horns of buffaloes are used for protection and can reach up to two feet in length.
- Buffaloes have an incredibly strong sense of smell, and can detect scents from up to a mile away.
- Buffaloes are an important source of food for many communities around the world.

BUTTERFLIES AND MOTHS

BUTTERFLIES AND MOTHS are some of the most amazing creatures in the animal kingdom. Their ability to camouflage themselves and metamorphose from caterpillars into beautiful butterflies is an astonishing process that never fails to amaze.

- Butterflies have been around for over 50 million years, making them one of the oldest living species on the planet.
- There are approximately 20,000 species of butterflies.
- Butterflies and moths have four wings covered in scales that overlap, which gives them a colorful appearance and helps them fly.
- Butterflies taste with their feet.
- The lifespan of a butterfly ranges from a few days to a few months, depending on the species.
- Moths are nocturnal, unlike butterflies which are usually active during the day.
- A butterfly's wings can beat up to 250 times per second.

- The migratory monarch butterfly can travel up to 3,000 miles during its migration cycle.
- Many species of butterflies and moths have the ability to taste with their antennae.
- Butterflies use their proboscis to drink nectar from flowers.
- Some species of moths have ears on their wings, allowing them to detect the ultrasonic sounds of bats.
- Monarch butterflies have a unique symbiotic relationship with the milkweed plant, using it to lay their eggs and feed their larvae.
- Butterflies have the ability to detect ultraviolet light, which helps them locate food and navigate during migration.
- Moths pollinate plants, just like bees and other insects.
- Some species of butterflies and moths can produce sounds by fluttering their wings.

CAMELS

CAMELS ARE incredible animals with many amazing qualities. They are well adapted to their environment, have an incredible ability to store water and energy reserves, can carry heavy loads and have an extraordinary sense of smell and hearing. Here are some amazing facts about camels:

- Camels can close their nostrils to keep sand out.
- Camels can smell water from miles away.
- Camels can drink up to 30 gallons of water in one sitting.
- Camels can go for more than two weeks without food or water.
- Camels can hold their breath for up to 40 minutes.
- Camels can produce up to three gallons of saliva a day.
- Camels can survive temperatures as low as -4 degrees Fahrenheit.
- Camels can run up to 25 miles per hour.
- Camels have two rows of eyelashes to keep out sand.
- Camels can stick out their tongue to help cool off.

- Camels have been domesticated for over 5,000 years.
- Camels can live up to 40 years.
- Camels have three sets of eyelids to protect their eyes from the sun.
- Camels can produce a third more milk than cows.
- Camels can travel up to 100 miles in one day.

CATS

SEE ALSO: BIG CATS

CATS ARE TRULY AMAZING ANIMALS. They can sleep for up to 16 hours a day, purr at a frequency known to promote healing, and can jump up to 6 times their own height. Here are some more interesting facts about cats:

- Cats can run at speeds of up to 31 miles per hour.
- Cats can make over one hundred vocal sounds, while dogs can only make around ten.
- Cats can rotate their ears 180 degrees.
- Cats can see in the dark and have a wider field of view than humans.
- Cats have an excellent sense of balance, thanks to their long tails, which act as a counterbalance.
- Cats have whiskers on the back of their front legs to help them navigate in the dark.
- Cats have a strong sense of smell, which is 14 times better than that of humans.
- Cats have a third eyelid, called a nictitating membrane, which helps keep their eyes moist and protected.

- Domestic cats can taste sweetness, unlike most other mammals.
- Cats can hear sounds up to two octaves higher than humans.
- A single cat can have as many as 24 different types of muscles in its ears.
- Cats have a special membrane in their cheeks which allows them to suck up liquids without using their tongues.
- A cat's heart beats twice as fast as a human heart, at up to 140 beats per minute.
- Cats are able to survive falls from great heights without serious injury.

CHEETAHS

CHEETAHS ARE the fastest land animals on the planet with the ability to reach speeds of up to 75 mph. They have exceptional eyesight which allows them to spot potential prey from up to 5 km away and they can accelerate from 0 to 60 mph in just three seconds.

- Cheetahs have spotted coats which act as camouflage in their natural habitat.
- Cheetahs are very agile and can turn quickly while running due to their semi-retractable claws.
- Cheetahs have exceptionally good eyesight and can spot potential prey from up to 5 km away.
- Cheetahs are carnivores, mainly eating small antelopes and gazelles.
- Cheetahs can live for up to 12 years in the wild and up to 17 years in captivity.
- Cheetahs are diurnal (active during the day) animals.
- Cheetahs live in a variety of habitats, including grasslands, savannas and open woodlands.

- Cheetahs use their tails as a steering wheel while they are running.
- Cheetahs have long bodies and short legs.
- Cheetahs cannot roar like other big cats such as lions and tigers, but they can purr.
- Cheetahs are the only big cats that are unable to fully retract their claws.
- Cheetahs are solitary animals and live alone or in small family groups.

CHICKENS

CHICKENS ARE fascinating animals which have been domesticated for thousands of years. They come in many different breeds, shapes, and sizes, and are capable of some remarkable feats! Here are some amazing facts about chickens:

- Chickens are able to distinguish between more than 100 different types of sounds.
- Chickens can recognize their owners and can even remember up to 100 different faces.
- A rooster can crow up to 150 times a day.
- Hens are able to lay up to 200 eggs per year.
- Chickens have poor eyesight but they have a strong sense of smell and hearing.
- Chickens can fly short distances and can reach speeds up to 9 mph.
- Chickens have a unique behavior called "dust bathing," which is how they keep themselves clean.
- Chickens are omnivores and will eat a variety of food including plants, fruits and insects.
- Chickens can live up to 10 years.

- A female chicken is called a hen and a male chicken is called a rooster.
- Chickens have a pecking order which is determined by age and size.
- Hens will sometimes turn eggs in the nest to ensure even incubation.
- Roosters have large combs on top of their heads which can be up to 6 inches tall.
- Chickens can live in temperatures as cold as -20 degrees Fahrenheit.
- Hens are able to produce the same cackle when they lay an egg.

CHIMPANZEES

CHIMPANZEES ARE one of the most intelligent species on earth and can be found in the wild in parts of Africa. They are incredibly social creatures, living and interacting in groups of up to 150 individuals. They are also incredibly strong, able to lift objects five times their own body weight.

- Chimpanzees use tools to solve problems and gather food, such as extracting honey.
- They can recognize themselves in a mirror.
- In certain areas, chimps have been observed using spears to hunt.
- They have complex communication systems which involve facial expressions, vocalizations, and body language.
- Chimpanzees share 98.7% of their DNA with humans.
- Chimpanzees are among the few species which have been observed to make and use medicine.
- They are highly adept climbers, capable of scaling trees and other large objects.

- They have individual personalities with different strengths and weaknesses.
- Chimpanzees can live for up to 60 years in the wild.
- Mothers teach their young specific skills and behaviors.
- They can learn sign language and have been observed using it to communicate with humans.
- Chimpanzees have been observed using rocks to crack open nuts.
- Chimpanzees are capable of planning ahead and problem-solving.

CLAMS

CLAMS, also known as bivalves, are a fascinating species of molluscs found in a variety of water habitats. These adaptable creatures are renowned for their incredible burrowing abilities, and their unique anatomy, which includes two hinged shells. Here are some incredible facts about clams:

- Clams can live for more than 100 years.
- Clams use two separate siphons to draw in water and to expel waste.
- Clams can sense vibrations and changes in water pressure.
- Clams have a specialised organ called the 'statocyst' which helps them to maintain balance.
- Clams have one of the most powerful digging muscles in the animal kingdom.
- Clams can close their shells with a force of up to 20 pounds per square inch.
- Clams are filter feeders and feed on tiny organisms in the water. They can filter up to 2L of water per hour.

- Clams have a specialised organ called the 'mantle' which is used for breathing and excreting waste.
- Clams can move by using a wave-like motion of their foot muscle.
- Clams are hermaphrodites and are capable of producing sperm and eggs simultaneously.
- Clams can produce pearls when a foreign object is trapped in their shells.
- Clams can change colour according to their environment.
- Clams are an important source of food for many aquatic animals.

COCKROACHES

COCKROACHES ARE some of the most resilient creatures on Earth, with an amazing array of adaptations that have allowed them to survive for millions of years. They can withstand incredibly hot and cold temperatures, survive for weeks without food, and even live without their heads for weeks! Here are some amazing facts about cockroaches:

- Cockroaches can run up to three miles an hour.
- Cockroaches can hold their breath for up to 40 minutes.
- Cockroaches have adapted to survive in virtually any environment, from Arctic cold to tropical heat.
- Cockroaches can squeeze through spaces as small as 1/16th of an inch.
- Cockroaches secrete a natural repellent that keeps predators away.
- Cockroaches are able to survive radiation up to 15 times higher than humans.
- Cockroaches can survive for up to two weeks underwater.

- Cockroaches can go without oxygen for up to 45 minutes.
- Cockroaches can eat almost anything and have even been known to eat books.
- Cockroaches have a lifespan of up to one year in the wild.
- Cockroaches have three sets of eyelids.
- Cockroaches can grow up to four inches in length.

CORALS

CORALS ARE fascinating organisms that are integral to the health of oceans and the diversity of marine life. A single coral reef can be home to up to 25% of the world's fish species, and some species of coral can live for over 100 years! Here are some amazing facts about corals:

- Corals are actually colonies of thousands of small animals called polyps that are connected to one another.
- The color of a coral comes from the symbiotic algae that live in its tissue.
- When conditions become too warm, corals can expel the symbiotic algae living in their tissues, causing them to turn completely white, a process known as coral bleaching.
- There are over 600 species of stony coral and over 300 species of soft coral.
- Coral reefs are the most diverse of all marine ecosystems.
- Coral reefs can grow at rates of up to 4 cm (1.6 in) per year.

- Corals are found in all oceans, but the most well-known reefs are located in the Caribbean, Red Sea, and the Great Barrier Reef in Australia.
- Reefs provide habitats for many species of fish and other animals, such as sea turtles, starfish, and crabs.
- Some species of coral can reproduce asexually by splitting into two separate colonies.
- The oldest known coral is estimated to be 8,000 to 10,000 years old.
- Corals reproduce by releasing eggs and sperm into the water at the same time, which then join together to form larvae.
- Corals provide food and shelter to thousands of species of fish and other animals.
- Corals can be used to monitor changes in ocean temperature and acidification due to climate change. They are highly sensitive to changes in water temperature, pollution, and other environmental factors.
- Corals are important for healthy oceans and contribute to the global economy by generating tourism and fisheries revenue.

COWS

COWS ARE amazing animals with many unique facts and abilities. They can live up to 20 years and produce 120 liters of milk per day. They spend 6-7 hours a day eating and 8-10 hours ruminating and are incredibly social, forming strong bonds with other cows in their herd. Here are some more amazing facts about cows:

- Cows can produce up to 8 gallons (30 liters) of saliva per day.
- Cows have almost 360-degree panoramic vision, allowing them to observe predators from almost any direction.
- Cows can lick up to 40 times per minute.
- Cows have 32 teeth, but no upper front teeth.
- Cows have an excellent sense of smell and can detect smells up to 6 miles away.
- Cows can hear very low frequencies, up to 80 Hz, which is lower than the human ear can detect.
- Cows can drink up to 25-50 gallons (95-190 liters) of water per day.

- Cows have four stomachs which help them digest their food.
- Cows can walk up and down stairs, but not jump.
- Cows can run at speeds of up to 25 miles per hour.
- Cows can recognize and remember up to 100 other cows in their herd.
- Cows can understand certain commands and can even respond to their name when called.
- Cows can live up to 20 years and produce milk for their entire life.
- Cows are the most commonly farmed livestock in the world, with close to 1 billion cows around the world.

CRABS AND CRUSTACEANS

CRABS AND CRUSTACEANS are incredible creatures, possessing unique characteristics and adapted to a variety of environments. They are incredibly hardy, with some species living over a hundred years and being able to survive extreme environments. Here are some amazing facts about crabs and crustaceans.

- Crabs and crustaceans can regrow lost limbs and even vital organs.
- Crabs are capable of making intricate tools with the claws and legs to acquire food or protect themselves.
- Many crustacean species are capable of surviving in an anoxic state, allowing them to survive in environments with limited oxygen.
- Crabs and crustaceans can survive freezing temperatures and can even produce proteins that act as antifreeze in their muscles.
- Crabs and crustaceans have compound eyes, allowing them to see in multiple directions at once.
- Crabs and crustaceans can be omnivorous, herbivorous, and even carnivorous.

- Crabs and crustaceans have gills to breathe underwater and can absorb oxygen from the water for respiration.
- Crabs and crustaceans can use the same body parts for different functions, such as using their legs for swimming.
- Crabs and crustaceans can communicate with each other through drumming, stridulation, and visual cues.
- Crabs and crustaceans have an exoskeleton made of chitin, which is incredibly strong and helps them to survive in their environment.
- Crabs and crustaceans have a wide range of colors and patterns on their carapaces and can even use camouflage to hide from predators.
- Crabs and crustaceans have powerful claws and legs that can be used to defend against predators.
- Crabs and crustaceans can use tools and learn behaviors, such as learning how to open containers to get food.
- Crabs and crustaceans have adapted to live in almost any water environment, from the ocean to freshwater streams.
- Crabs and crustaceans can live in brackish and salty water, with some species surviving in both freshwater and saltwater.

CROWS

SEE ALSO: RAVENS

CROWS ARE INCREDIBLY intelligent birds with complex social behaviors, amazing problem-solving skills, and even an impressive memory. They are incredibly adaptable to their environment and can learn to recognize individual humans and animals. They have been observed using tools.

- Crows are found all over the world, except in the polar regions.
- Crows can recognize individual humans and animals.
- They can communicate with one another in a variety of ways, such as cawing, posturing, and other vocalizations. Crows have an impressive range of vocalizations and can make more than 250 distinct sounds.
- Crows are very social and live in large, complex groups called "murders" or "roosts."
- Crows can remember things for several years, even if they only encounter them a few times.
- Their diet consists of insects, small mammals, eggs, fruit, and grain.

- Crows are very protective of their nests and will warn other members of their family when there is a potential threat.
- Crows have been observed using sticks, rocks, and other objects to pick up food or attract mates.
- Crows have been known to engage in playful behavior, such as sliding down snowbanks or dropping objects into water and watching the splash.
- Crows can live up to 14 years in the wild.
- Crows have excellent eyesight and are able to spot small prey from high above.
- Crows mate for life and stay together for years.

DOGS

DOGS ARE AMAZING ANIMALS, capable of understanding a wide variety of complex behaviors. They can be loyal and loving companions, as well as incredibly intelligent. Here are some amazing facts about them:

- Dogs have more than 300 million olfactory receptors, compared with 6 million in humans.
- Some breeds, such as the Border collie, can learn up to 250 commands.
- Dogs can sense very small changes in the Earth's magnetic field.
- Dogs can identify human emotions by examining the tone, pitch and volume of a person's voice.
- Dogs can do simple math, such as recognizing the relationship between two different numbers.
- Dogs can detect the presence of diseases in humans.
- Dogs can understand pointing and gesturing better than chimpanzees.
- Dogs can remember events for up to five years.
- Dogs have a sense of time and are able to recognize the difference between intervals of time.

- Dogs can recognize different human faces and remember them for years.
- Dogs can detect changes in barometric pressure, which makes them good predictors of the weather.
- Dogs can be trained to detect explosives, drugs, and other contraband.
- Dogs can detect diseases such as malaria, diabetes, and even certain types of cancer through smell alone.

DOLPHINS

DOLPHINS ARE TRULY INCREDIBLE CREATURES. They are highly intelligent, sociable, and very adaptable. Dolphins have a unique form of communication, a sophisticated system of echolocation, and many species can live in both freshwater and saltwater. Here are some amazing facts about dolphins:

- Dolphins can hold their breath for up to 8 minutes.
- Dolphins are able to recognize themselves in a mirror.
- Dolphins can understand basic commands, signals and gestures from humans.
- Dolphins can swim up to 20 miles per hour.
- Some dolphins have lived for over 50 years.
- Dolphins have a unique form of communication, including clicks and whistles.
- Bottlenose dolphins form lifelong bonds with their friends and family.
- Dolphins use echolocation to locate objects in the water.

- Mothers teach their young how to find food, take care of themselves, and even how to play.
- Dolphins are very curious and playful and often use objects to play with each other.
- The oldest known dolphin species is the Boto, which dates back over 15 million years.
- Bottlenose dolphins can change the pitch of their whistles to communicate with each other.
- Dolphins have a complex social structure and are often seen cooperating with each other.
- Dolphins are highly adaptable and are able to live in both fresh and salt water.
- Dolphins have been observed helping humans in distress, and guiding lost swimmers back to shore.

INTERLUDE: ANIMAL CAMOUFLAGE

Animal camouflage is an amazing phenomenon. Animals have adapted to their habitats in ways that allow them to blend in with the environment, giving them great survival advantage. Here are some amazing facts about animal camouflage:

- Chameleons are able to match the color of their skin to the color of their surroundings in as little as 20 seconds.
- Moths have evolved to blend in with the bark of trees to avoid being noticed by predators.
- Some butterflies have evolved to look like dead leaves so that they can hide in plain sight.

- Many species of fish have developed patterns that mimic the reflection of sun on the ocean surface.
- Stick insects have evolved to look like the twigs they live on, perfectly matching the shape, color, and texture of their environment.
- Many species of frogs and toads have evolved to match the color of the leaves and rocks in their environment.
- Some species of spiders have developed the ability to change their color to match the color of their environment.
- The polar bear has evolved to be nearly white in order to blend in with their snowy surroundings.
- The snow leopard has spots that resemble rocks, allowing it to blend in with its rocky mountain environment.
- The flounder has evolved to blend in perfectly with the sandy sea floor to avoid predators.
- Many species of birds, such as the mallard, have evolved to blend in with the background in order to hide from predators.
- The Arctic fox has evolved to have white fur in the winter and brown fur in the summer, allowing it to blend in with its environment in any season.
- The pygmy seahorse mimics the color and pattern of the coral it lives in, making it incredibly difficult for predators to spot.
- The Texas blind snake has evolved to look like a worm, helping it avoid being spotted by predators.

DRAGONFLIES

DRAGONFLIES ARE FASCINATING CREATURES! These amazing creatures can fly up to 30 miles per hour, have four wings that beat 30 times per second, and can see in all directions even when their heads are facing forward. They can live up to 6 months and even fly backwards. Here are some more amazing facts about dragonflies:

- The average dragonfly has four wings, each with over 10,000 individual facets.
- Dragonflies can detect ultraviolet light and use it to communicate.
- They can eat up to 1000 mosquito-sized insects a day.
- In some species, female dragonflies have the ability to store sperm for later use.
- The largest dragonfly species have wingspans that can reach up to 7.5 inches.
- Most dragonflies live for only a few weeks to a few months.
- Dragonflies have a lifespan of two to four weeks depending on the species and conditions.

- Dragonflies have the ability to hover and fly forward, backward, and sideways.
- The eyes of dragonflies are made up of 30,000 individual lenses.
- The larvae of dragonflies can take up to three years to mature.
- Dragonflies feed on various flying insects, including mosquitoes, moths, and midges.
- Dragonflies can see in all directions, even when their heads are facing forward.
- Some dragonfly species migrate long distances in order to reproduce.

DUCKS AND GEESE

SEE ALSO: SWANS

DUCKS and geese are some of the most interesting and amazing birds in the world. They have a range of unique abilities and behaviours which make them fascinating to observe and study. Some examples of their amazing abilities include the ability to fly long distances, migrate every year, and even stay underwater for long periods of time. Not only are they incredibly resilient, but they are also remarkably intelligent and social creatures that form tight bonds with one another.

- Ducks, geese and swans are all members of the Anatidae family.
- They are found around the world in both temperate and tropical climates.
- They have webbed feet which help them to swim and forage for food in water, and feathers that keep them waterproof.
- Ducks and geese are excellent fliers, and some species can even travel long distances during annual migration. They are able to fly up to 60 miles per hour.

- They can dive underwater to search for food, and some species can stay underwater for as long as two minutes.
- They can all drink either fresh or saltwater.
- Male ducks are known for their vibrant plumage, often used to attract mates during courtship.
- Ducks and geese nest on the ground, with some species sometimes nesting in trees or shrubs.
- Ducks and geese can live up to 25 years in the wild.
- They have specially designed bills that help them to filter food from water.
- They can all be found feeding in the same areas, and some species are even known to form mixed flocks.
- They can 'stretch' their neck out when searching for food in shallow water.
- They are highly social animals and can often be seen preening, bathing and playing with each other.
- They are all very vocal birds, with different species making a variety of different sounds.
- Ducks and geese have a gland near their tails that helps them expel excess water.

ELEPHANTS

ELEPHANTS ARE one of the most fascinating animals in the world. They are the largest land animals, with males reaching heights of up to 13 feet and weighing up to 14,000 pounds. Their unique features and behaviors make them truly amazing. Here are some amazing facts about elephants:

- Elephants have the longest gestation period of any land mammal, lasting up to 22 months.
- Elephants have an excellent memory and can remember experiences and places they've been to many years later.
- Elephants are highly social and live in close-knit family groups of up to 10 members.
- Elephants produce a wide range of sounds, including infrasonic calls that can travel up to 6 miles.
- Elephants can use their trunk to recognize smells and pick up objects as small as a single blade of grass.
- Elephants have the largest brains of any land animal.

- Elephants can recognize themselves in a mirror due to their high intelligence.
- Elephants sleep between 3 and 4 hours each day.
- Elephants are capable of swimming, and can hold their breath for up to 6 minutes underwater.
- Elephants have excellent vision and can see color.
- Elephants are the only animal that can use their tusks to dig for water.
- Elephant skin can be up to 4 inches thick in some areas.
- Elephants use mud baths to stay cool and protect their skin from the sun.
- Elephants can live up to 70 years in the wild.
- Elephants are herbivores, and can eat up to 300 pounds of vegetation in a single day.

EMUS

EMUS ARE the second-largest bird species in the world and are native to Australia. These tall, flightless birds are able to reach speeds of up to 30 miles per hour and have powerful legs that enable them to swim as well as run.

- Emus can reach a height of up to two meters tall.
- They have three stomachs.
- Emus have double-plumed feathers that are soft and brown in colour.
- They are able to survive in a wide range of habitats, from the arid desert to the wet tropics.
- Emus can travel long distances in search of food.
- They are omnivorous and eat a variety of foods, including plants, insects, and small animals.
- Emus have long necks and small heads.
- They have a long, curved beak that they use to pluck food from the ground.
- Emus have powerful legs that enable them to swim as well as run.
- They can reach speeds of up to 30 miles per hour.

- Adult emus communicate with each other through a series of low grunting sounds.
- Emus lay eggs that are green in colour.
- Emu chicks are able to stand and walk almost immediately after hatching.
- Emus are able to live for up to 10 years in the wild.
- Emus are able to jump as high as seven feet in the air, being the only birds with calf muscles.

FIREFLIES

FIREFLIES, also known as lightning bugs, are a type of beetle. They are known for their glowing abdomens, which are created by a chemical reaction that produces light. Fireflies are found on every continent, except Antarctica, and can be seen in the summertime in many places around the world.

- Fireflies produce light through a natural chemical reaction inside their abdomens.
- The reaction is called bioluminescence and is used by fireflies to communicate with each other.
- Fireflies use their light to attract mates and warn other fireflies of danger.
- There are over 2000 species of fireflies around the world.
- Fireflies can flash their lights in different patterns to identify themselves.
- Fireflies are typically nocturnal and can live for several weeks.
- Adult fireflies eat nectar and pollen, while larvae feed on other insects.

- Fireflies produce hormone called lucibufagins, which are a mild toxin that can ward off predators.
- Some species of firefly can flash their light continuously for up to four hours.
- Fireflies are located on every continent in the world except Antarctica.
- The largest firefly species is the Malaysian Jack O'Lantern firefly, which can grow up to two inches long.
- Fireflies can produce a bright light without producing any heat.
- The light produced by a firefly is so efficient that almost all of the energy used is converted into light.
- Fireflies are also used as a natural pest control as they can eat up to 1000 mosquitoes in one night.
- Fireflies are declining in numbers due to light pollution, habitat destruction, and the use of pesticides.

FISH

SEE ALSO: PUFFERFISH, SEAHORSES, SHARKS, STARFISH

FISH ARE INCREDIBLY DIVERSE, with over 33,000 known species. Many of these fish are capable of remarkable adaptations to their environments, making for some truly amazing facts about them.

- The giant ocean sunfish is the largest bony fish in the world, growing to as much as 4.3 meters in length.
- The opah is the first fish discovered to be fully warm-blooded.
- The elephantnose fish uses electric fields to find its prey.
- Some fish can survive in extremely cold waters, as low as -2°C.
- The Australian lungfish can breathe air while out of water and can stay out of water for up to four days.
- The seahorse is the only fish with a neck.
- The spotted handfish can use its fins to 'walk' on the sea floor.
- The barreleye fish has an almost transparent head and its eyes can rotate within its transparent dome.

- The Atlantic stargazer can bury itself in the sand and can create electric fields to stun its prey.
- The coelacanth is considered a living fossil as it has remained unchanged for 400 million years.
- The mudskipper can survive out of water for up to five days.
- The bowfin can breathe air using its swim bladder.
- The archerfish can spit jets of water to knock its prey out of trees.
- The arapaima can gulp air to survive in oxygen-poor waters.
- The red-lipped batfish uses its fins to 'walk' on the sea floor.

FLIES

SEE ALSO: BUTTERFLIES, FIREFLIES

FLIES ARE INCREDIBLE CREATURES, full of surprises. Despite their small size, they are incredibly resilient and resourceful. Not only are they remarkable flyers, but they also have the ability to taste with their feet and detect movement up to 50 times faster than other animals! Here are some amazing facts about flies:

- A fly can take off and stop in less than one third of a second.
- Flies can see ultraviolet light.
- They can taste with their feet.
- Some species of flies can fly up to 14 miles in a single day.
- Female houseflies can lay up to 500 eggs in one batch.
- Some fly species have a lifespan of only a few hours.
- Flies can detect and avoid obstacles while flying at almost any speed.
- Flies have four eyes, two large compound eyes, and three small simple eyes.

- Some fly species can live in temperatures as low as -58 degrees Fahrenheit.
- Flies have the ability to detect motion up to 50 times faster than humans.
- Flies can survive for up to 24 hours underwater.
- Flies can fly at up to 15 miles per hour.
- Flies can change direction mid-flight at speeds up to 180 times per second.
- Flies can survive up to a month without food.
- Flies can carry up to 600 times their body weight.

FOXES

FOXES ARE AMAZING ANIMALS, with many unique characteristics. They have keen senses of hearing, smell, and sight, and are also highly intelligent. They are also well-adapted for their habitat, and have a number of unique features that allow them to survive and thrive in the wild. Here are some amazing facts about foxes:

- Foxes are omnivores, eating small mammals, birds, reptiles, insects, fruits, and even eggs.
- Foxes have remarkable hearing, able to detect the faintest of sounds up to a mile away.
- Foxes possess a distinctive trotting gait, enabling them to quickly traverse their environment.
- Foxes can be found in almost every continent in the world, except Antarctica and a few remote islands.
- Foxes have pointed muzzles, large ears, and a long, bushy tail that helps to keep them warm in cold weather.
- Foxes communicate with each other through a variety of vocalizations, including barks, growls, and screams.

- The red fox is the largest of the fox species, weighing up to 15 pounds with a body length of up to three feet.
- Foxes have excellent eyesight, enabling them to spot their prey from far distances.
- Foxes have remarkable agility, able to jump up to six feet in the air and dive underground to catch prey.
- Foxes are active mainly during night time, but can also be seen during the day.
- Foxes live in small family groups, with an adult male and female leading the pack.
- Foxes have a wide range of predators, including wolves, coyotes, lynxes, and humans.
- Foxes have a special layer of fur called the winter coat, which helps to keep them warm during colder temperatures.
- Foxes can be found in a variety of habitats, including forests, grasslands, mountains, and even urban areas.
- Foxes use the earth's magnetic field to help them navigate their environment.

FROGS AND TOADS

FROGS AND TOADS are some of the most fascinating creatures, with a wide range of special adaptations and behaviours. They can be found in both warm and cold climates, and come in a variety of shapes and sizes. From the tiny bronze frog to the giant goliath frog, each species has something special to offer. Here are some amazing facts about frogs and toads:

- Some frog species can lay up to 3,000 eggs in a single clutch.
- Frogs and toads have an excellent sense of hearing, which helps them find food, evade predators, and communicate with each other.
- They can jump incredibly high, up to 20 times their own body length, using their powerful legs and webbed feet.
- They have a wide variety of colorations, from bright green to dark brown or even a speckled pattern. Some can change their skin color to blend in with the environment and hide from predators.

- Frogs are able to close their nostrils and ears when they are underwater.
- Frogs and toads have long tongues that they can use to catch and swallow their prey.
- They have vocal sacs that produce a wide range of sounds to attract mates and ward off predators.
- They can use their eyes independently of each other, allowing them to look in two directions at once.
- They have a third eye called the parietal eye, located on top of their heads, that helps them detect changes in light.
- Frogs and toads can breathe through their skin, as well as their lungs, which helps them stay underwater for extended periods of time.
- They can detect vibrations and signals in the ground with pressure receptors located in their feet and legs.
- Some frogs and toads can glide through the air, using their webbed feet to steer and slow their descent.
- Frogs and toads have a unique anatomy that allows them to swallow their prey whole, without having to chew it.
- Frogs and toads have no tail, unlike most other amphibians.
- Frogs and toads are capable of regenerating lost body parts, such as a limb or an eye.

GARDEN BIRDS

SEE ALSO: OWLS, BIRDS OF PREY

GARDEN BIRDS ARE TRULY remarkable creatures – their diverse colourings, adaptability and resourcefulness can be a joy to behold. Here are some amazing facts about them:

- Though most garden birds are active during the day, some species, like owls, are nocturnal.
- The waxwing is a type of garden bird which moves south from Scandinavia in search of food in winter.
- Garden birds often use mud to construct their nests.
- The house sparrows, which are common in many gardens, have been around for almost 10,000 years.
- Some garden birds use mimicry to copy the calls of other species and attract a mate.
- Nuthatches are adept climbers that can walk head first down trees.
- Some garden birds, such as starlings, can produce complex and beautiful song.
- Robins are territorial and will often return to the same nesting site year after year.
- Blue tits and great tits are intelligent birds that can learn to open milk bottles and even bird feeders.

- The male blackbird is quite territorial and will often fight other males off to protect its territory.
- Wrens are small but powerful birds that can fly up to 15 miles per hour.
- The black cap is a species of garden bird which can imitate the call of other species.
- Some garden birds, such as swallows, can cover long distances in order to migrate for the winter.
- Woodpeckers use their beaks to peck into trees and tree trunks in order to forage for food.
- The chiffchaff is a small garden bird which can copy the calls of other species in order to ward off predators.

GIRAFFES

GIRAFFES ARE some of the most remarkable animals on the planet. Their long necks, spotted coats, and impressive height make them truly one-of-a-kind. Here are some amazing facts about giraffes:

- Giraffes can run at speeds of up to 35 miles per hour.
- They are the tallest land animal, with an average height of 17-20 feet.
- Giraffes have special valves in their neck to regulate their blood pressure.
- Giraffes have the same number of vertebrae as humans – 7 in the neck and 12-15 in the spine.
- Giraffes use their tongues to eat leaves from trees, which can measure up to 21 inches long.
- Their long legs allow them to reach heights of up to 18 feet to eat leaves from tall trees.
- Giraffes live up to 25 years in the wild and even longer in captivity.
- Giraffes use a unique form of communication called 'giraffing' – a series of low-frequency sounds.

- Giraffes are herbivores, meaning they only eat plants.
- Female giraffes give birth while standing up and their offspring can stand and walk within an hour of being born.
- Giraffes have large, cloven hooves, which help them walk on soft sand.
- Giraffes only need 5-30 minutes of sleep in a 24-hour period.
- Giraffes have unique fur patterns, like fingerprints, making each individual giraffe easily distinguishable.
- Giraffe calves are about 6 feet tall when born.
- Giraffes have two distinct layers of fur, with thick underfur and long, course guard hairs.

GOATS

GOATS ARE some of the most versatile animals on the planet and they have been used as a source of food, tools and even as therapy animals. They are intelligent and social animals which are able to learn complex tasks, recognize their owners and even use tools. Here are some of their amazing abilities and traits:

- Goats can be taught their name and to come when called.
- Goats can be trained to pull carts and carry packs of light supplies.
- They are able to distinguish between different facial expressions.
- They have rectangular pupils which give them a wide range of vision.
- They have the ability to climb and jump incredibly high.
- Goats are great swimmers and have been seen crossing rivers and streams.
- They have four stomachs to help them digest their food.

- They have cloven hooves which help them to keep their balance on difficult terrain.
- They can remember the location of food sources for up to five years.
- Goats can recognize the voice of their owners and respond to them.
- Goats can learn behaviors faster when they are rewarded with food or treats.
- They can be trained to help with household chores, like closing doors.
- Goats can live for up to 15 years when kept in a safe environment.

GORILLAS

GORILLAS ARE INCREDIBLY INTELLIGENT CREATURES, capable of communicating with each other through a variety of vocalizations, facial expressions, and hand gestures. They have an impressive range of emotion, and can form strong bonds with one another. Gorillas have been known to demonstrate a wide range of problem-solving capabilities, and are capable of using tools to reach food.

- Gorillas are the world's largest primates, weighing up to 400 pounds.
- Gorillas can climb trees up to 30 feet tall.
- They live in troops of up to 30 individuals, led by a They male silverback.
- Gorillas build nests in trees to sleep in at night.
- Gorillas are mostly vegetarians, eating mostly leafy plants, fruits, and roots.
- They are native to sub-Saharan Africa, living in the forests of Rwanda, Uganda, and the Democratic Republic of Congo.
- Gorillas can live up to 50 years in the wild.

- On average, gorillas are four times stronger than humans.
- Gorillas have a non-hierarchical social structure, with females making up the majority of the troop.
- They have a complex vocal communication system, including grunts, screams, and roars.
- They can recognize themselves in a mirror.
- Gorillas can use tools to reach food and other items.
- Gorillas have been known to mourn the death of a troop mate.
- Gorillas are critically endangered due to habitat loss and poaching.

GUINEA PIGS

GUINEA PIGS ARE one of the most popular animals to keep as pets, and with good reason! They are incredibly intelligent, social, and fun animals that can bring joy to their owners. Here are some amazing facts about these fascinating creatures:

- Guinea pigs can live up to 8 years when well-cared for.
- They can learn their name and come when they are called.
- Guinea pigs don't have any teeth on their top jaw, but they still enjoy crunchy vegetables like carrots.
- They can make a variety of noises including purring, chirping, and squeaking.
- Male guinea pigs have a special scent gland on their forehead used to mark their territory.
- Some guinea pigs can learn to use a litter box.
- They can't make their own Vitamin C, so it needs to be supplemented in their diet.
- Guinea pigs have a special way of communicating by doing a "popcorning" dance when they are excited.

- They are herbivores, meaning they only eat plant-based food.
- Guinea pigs can sleep with one eye open to stay alert for danger.
- They can run up to speeds of 5 miles per hour.
- They have poor eyesight but an acute sense of smell.
- Guinea pigs love to explore and play, so providing them with lots of toys is important.
- They have a three-chambered stomach which helps them digest their food more efficiently.
- They enjoy interacting with their owners and make great companions.

HAMSTERS

HAMSTERS ARE SMALL, cute and furry, and they make great pets. They are also quite amazing creatures, with a variety of interesting characteristics and behaviors. Here are some amazing facts about hamsters:

- Hamsters breed quickly and can produce several litters in a year.
- Hamsters can run as fast as four and a half miles per hour.
- Hamsters are colorblind but can see ultraviolet light.
- Hamsters have a unique "sleep cycle", which involves periods of activity during the day, and periods of inactivity during the night.
- Hamsters have large cheek pouches that they use to store food and bedding.
- Hamsters have retractable claws to help them dig.
- Hamsters can store up to 30% of their body weight in food in their cheeks.
- Hamsters have a unique sense of smell and can detect food from long distances.

- Hamsters have poor eyesight but their sense of hearing is very acute.
- Hamsters can remember paths to food sources and are good navigators.
- Hamsters are natural hoarders and they like to hide food in their bedding.
- Hamsters are omnivores and will eat both plants and small animals.
- Hamsters use their whiskers to detect objects in the dark.
- Hamsters are nocturnal, meaning they are most active at night.
- Hamsters can live up to three years in captivity.

HARES

HARES ARE SURPRISINGLY VERSATILE ANIMALS, capable of remarkable feats of strength and agility. They can reach speeds of up to 45 mph, jump over 9 feet in a single bound, and survive harsh winter temperatures down to -40° Fahrenheit. They can also swim, live in a variety of habitats, and can even change the color of their fur to blend in with the environment.

- Hares can swim.
- They are well adapted to living in a variety of habitats.
- Hares can change the color of their fur to blend in with the environment.
- Hares are very territorial creatures.
- They can live up to 10 years in the wild.
- Hares are herbivores.
- Hares typically give birth to 2-4 offspring.
- The gestation period for hares is 42-45 days.
- Hares have a very good sense of hearing and smell.
- Hares have long ears and have excellent vision.

- Hares can reach lengths of up to 3 feet.
- Hares prefer to sleep during the day and are active at night.

HEDGEHOGS

HEDGEHOGS ARE INCREDIBLE CREATURES, with a variety of fascinating traits that make them unique among animals. They can sleep for up to 18 hours a day and have incredible homing abilities, able to return to their nest from distances up to a mile away. They are also able to climb trees, swim, and waddle through water.

- Hedgehogs can run at speeds of up to 4.5 mph.
- They have a keen sense of smell and hearing.
- They are able to curl up into a tight ball when feeling threatened.
- They have a life span of 3-6 years.
- They have a natural resistance to toxins and can eat venomous snakes and insects.
- Hedgehogs are nocturnal and active at night.
- They have a great memory and can recognize their owners.
- Hedgehogs have a unique tongue structure which is used to groom themselves.
- They are insectivores, eating mostly worms and insects.

- Hedgehogs have a loud snorting noise they make when disturbed.
- During the winter months, hedgehogs enter a state of hibernation.
- They are found in Europe, Africa, and Asia.
- Their spines are made of keratin, the same material that makes up human hair and nails.
- Hedgehogs have around 7,000 spines on their body.
- They are natural foragers and use their sense of smell to search for food.

HORSES

HORSES ARE TRULY remarkable animals with some incredible abilities. They can traverse a wide range of terrains, endure long distances and leap high fences with ease. They have an impressive capacity for learning and can even be taught to perform complex tasks. Here is a list of some amazing facts about horses:

- Horses can sleep both lying down and standing up.
- Horses can gallop at speeds of up to 55 mph.
- Wild horses live in groups called herds.
- Horses are able to see nearly 360 degrees around them.
- On average, horses live between 25 to 30 years.
- Horses can drink up to 10 gallons of water a day.
- Horses can recognize up to 100 human faces.
- Horses have one extra rib than humans, totaling 18 ribs.
- They are able to understand some basic human commands.
- They have the largest eyes of any land mammal.
- They are herbivores, meaning they only eat plants.

- Horses have three main gaits: walking, trotting, and galloping.
- They can tell the difference between their humans by scent.
- Horses have been used by humans for over 5,000 years.
- Horses have no upper front teeth, but have a hard pad instead.

HUMMINGBIRDS

HUMMINGBIRDS ARE one of nature's most amazing creatures. They possess the unique ability to hover in mid air, fly backwards, and even upside down! They are among the smallest of birds, yet they possess incredible strength and agility. Their tiny wings beat up to 80 times per second, allowing them to fly up to 30 mph and cover over 1,000 miles in migration.

- Hummingbirds are the smallest of all birds and can weigh as little as 2g.
- Hummingbirds can fly backwards and upside down.
- They have a very long tongue and can lap up nectar from some of the most difficult to reach places.
- Hummingbirds can hover in mid air.
- Hummingbirds can consume up to 8 times their body weight in nectar every day.
- In order to conserve energy, hummingbirds will go into a hibernation-like state known as torpor.
- They can fly as high as 10,000 feet.
- Hummingbirds can migrate over 1,000 miles.

- Hummingbirds have the ability to store fat in their tail and can use it for energy when needed.
- Hummingbirds can be found in almost every continent, except Antarctica and Europe.
- Hummingbirds have extraordinary vision and can even see ultraviolet light.
- Hummingbirds have a lifespan of about 5 years in the wild, but can live up to 10 years in captivity.
- Hummingbirds are the only birds that can also feed on insects as well as nectar.

HYENAS

HYENAS ARE some of the most interesting animals on the planet. They are intelligent, strong and resourceful, and they have a unique social structure. From their distinct laughing and whooping calls to their powerful hunting skills, hyenas are fascinating animals that are well worth learning about. Here are some amazing facts about hyenas:

- Hyenas are the largest members of the family Hyaenidae and the only species in the subfamily Hyaeninae.
- The most common hyena is the spotted hyena, which is native to sub-Saharan Africa.
- Hyenas live in clans with a complex social structure and a dominance hierarchy.
- Hyenas can run at speeds of up to 37 mph.
- Hyenas are excellent scavengers and can find food that other animals cannot.
- Although they look like dogs, hyenas are more closely related to cats.
- Female hyenas are larger and more aggressive than males.

- Spotted hyenas can live up to 20 years in the wild.
- Hyenas are highly intelligent, with the ability to solve complex puzzles.
- Hyenas feed on a variety of prey, including small mammals, birds, reptiles, and even carrion.
- Hyenas have an acute sense of smell and can detect prey from up to three miles away.
- Hyenas are highly social animals and communicate with each other through a variety of vocalizations.
- Hyenas have an incredible jaw strength and can crush bones with their powerful jaws.
- Hyenas can swim and use water to cool off during hot weather.
- Hyenas have a reputation for being sneaky, but they are actually quite brave and will stand their ground when threatened.

IBEXES

IBEXES ARE one of the most amazing animals in nature. Adapted for life in the harsh environments of the mountains, these agile creatures are incredibly strong and sure-footed. Not only can they climb sheer cliffs and maneuver on narrow ledges, but they can also leap over 9 feet high and 12 feet wide! Here are some amazing facts about ibexes:

- Ibexes can see up to three times better than humans in low light.
- Ibexes have special fur on their hooves that helps them grip rocky surfaces and steep slopes.
- They use their horns for defense, but also for sparring and for other forms of communication.
- Ibexes are the only wild goat species native to Europe.
- Ibexes are highly social animals, and will form large herds in the summer months.
- Ibexes have powerful hind legs and large, cloven hooves that help them climb steep slopes and traverse narrow ledges.

- Ibexes are well-adapted to extreme temperatures and can survive in temperatures as low as -51°F.
- Female ibexes are capable of producing two to three kids at a time.
- They can live up to 20 years in the wild.
- Ibexes have a long lifespan and strong family bonds that may continue for generations.
- Ibexes have a strong sense of smell, which helps them detect predators in their environment.
- Ibexes have a number of specialized physical adaptations, such as thick fur and double-layered coats, that help them survive in cold climates.
- Ibexes are browsers, meaning they feed on a variety of grasses, leaves, and other vegetation.
- Ibexes have been known to dig large holes in the ground in order to reach new pastures and find water.
- Ibexes are agile jumpers and can leap up to 9 feet high and 12 feet wide.

INSECTS

SEE ALSO: ANTS, BEES, COCKROACHES, FLIES, DRAGONFLIES, FIREFLIES, PRAYING MANTISES

INSECTS HAVE BEEN around for hundreds of millions of years, and are incredibly diverse and intriguing creatures. Their range of adaptations, behaviors, and structures is truly extraordinary. Here are some of the amazing facts about insects:

- Many insects can sense light with their antennae.
- The desert grasshopper can jump up to 30 times its own body length.
- Some species of beetles can live for up to seven years.
- Mosquitoes are one of the few flying insects that can taste their food.
- The Hercules beetle is the strongest insect, capable of lifting 850 times its own body weight.
- Leafcutter ants can carry up to fifty times their own body weight.
- Some moths have tongue-like organs that can reach up to 7 inches long.
- Stinkbugs can spray an unpleasant-smelling liquid up to three feet away.

JAGUARS

SEE ALSO: BIG CATS

JAGUARS ARE an impressive species of wild cats, ranging from the jungles of Central and South America to the woodlands of Arizona and New Mexico in the United States. They are the largest cats in the western hemisphere and are powerful swimmers and climbers. Here are some amazing facts about jaguars:

- Jaguars have one of the most powerful bites among big cats.
- Females typically weigh around 65 pounds while males can weigh as much as 160 pounds.
- Jaguars have a wide variety of prey, which include deer, wild pigs, crocodiles, snakes, and fish.
- Jaguar cubs are spotted at birth, but they lose their spots as they reach maturity.
- Jaguars have the ability to leap up to 20 feet.
- Jaguars are known to swim in the Amazon river and other bodies of water.
- Jaguars can reach speeds of up to 50 miles per hour.
- Jaguars may live up to 20 years in the wild.

- Jaguars are very territorial and can be fiercely protective of their hunting grounds.
- Jaguars are considered an endangered species due to habitat loss and poaching.
- The jaguar is the national animal of Guyana.
- Jaguars are an apex predator in their habitats.
- Jaguars have a unique rosette pattern on their coats.
- Jaguars are known to be solitary animals.
- Jaguars have a unique roar unlike other felines.

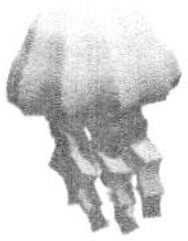

JELLYFISH

JELLYFISH ARE some of the most fascinating animals in the world. They are found all over the ocean, and come in a variety of shapes, sizes, and colors. They typically have a jelly-like bell-shape and tentacles that range in color from bright pink to blue. Jellyfish can live up to a year in the wild, and some species can survive in extreme temperatures. Here are some amazing facts about jellyfish:

- Some jellyfish are almost completely transparent.
- Jellyfish have no brains or hearts.
- Jellyfish can regenerate lost tentacles.
- There are over 2000 species of jellyfish.
- Jellyfish are older than the dinosaurs, with evidence of them living over 500 million years ago.
- Jellyfish can be deadly to humans, with some species having venom strong enough to kill an adult.
- Jellyfish can reproduce both sexually and asexually.
- Jellyfish can swim up to six feet per minute.
- A jellyfish's diet consists of plankton, small fish, and crustaceans.
- Some jellyfish can glow in the dark.

- Some jellyfish can live over 100 years.
- Jellyfish are a type of invertebrate, meaning they have no backbone.
- Jellyfish are made up of 95% water.
- Jellyfish can stop their heartbeat if they become dehydrated.
- Some jellyfish have as few as five tentacles, while others can have as many as 200.

KANGAROOS

KANGAROOS ARE one of the most fascinating animals on the planet. They are one of the few species of animals that can move by hopping, and their powerful legs help them to move quickly and jump high. They are also known for carrying their babies in a pouch, and for being great swimmers. Here is a list of some amazing facts about kangaroos:

- Kangaroos can move at up to 40 miles per hour.
- A group of kangaroos is known as a "mob".
- Kangaroos have very good vision, which helps them to spot predators from far away.
- Kangaroos sometimes use their tail to support themselves while standing up.
- A kangaroo can't walk backwards.
- Baby kangaroos are called joeys.
- Male kangaroos have a special pouch on their abdomen called a "brood pouch".
- A kangaroo's tail can be up to 1 meter long.
- Kangaroos are excellent swimmers.
- The kangaroo is Australia's national animal.
- The kangaroo's scientific name is Macropus.

- A kangaroo's powerful hind legs allow them to jump great distances.
- The gestation period for female kangaroos is about 33 days.
- Kangaroos can live up to 20 years.
- Kangaroos eat mostly grass and some leaves.

KOALAS

KOALAS ARE TRULY AMAZING CREATURES! Not only do they sleep for up to 20 hours a day, but they can also survive up to 50 days without drinking water. Here are some of their incredible characteristics:

- Koalas produce two different types of vocalizations – bellows and snores.
- They have two opposable digits on each of their front paws, which they use to grasp branches while climbing.
- Koalas are primarily herbivores, eating mostly eucalyptus leaves.
- Koalas have two thumbs on each front paw, as well as two toes on each rear paw.
- Koalas have a special pocket in their cheeks that allows them to store up to 30 eucalyptus leaves at a time.
- They have a slow metabolism and can survive up to 50 days without drinking water.
- They have a keen sense of smell which they use to detect food and identify other koalas.

- Koalas can sleep for up to 20 hours a day, conserving energy and resources.
- Females are larger than males, and can weigh up to 18 kilos.
- Koalas are marsupials, and their young are born undeveloped, living in the mother's pouch for the first 6-7 months of its life.
- Koalas have an extraordinary sense of hearing, with their ears moving independently and able to detect up to 50 different sounds.
- Koalas live in tall eucalyptus trees, and spend most of their time in branches up to 33 feet high.
- Koalas have a unique scent gland located on their chest which they use to mark their territory.
- They can reach speeds of up to 25 mph when in danger.
- Koalas have fingerprints which are unique to each individual and are used for identification.

LEMURS

LEMURS ARE some of the cutest and most interesting creatures on Earth. They are the only primates native to the island of Madagascar, where they live in the wild. These primates have some amazing adaptations that allow them to thrive in their environment. They come in a variety of sizes and colors, and they are capable of remarkable feats such as leaping great distances and navigating complex pathways. Here are some amazing facts about lemurs:

- Lemurs are the only primates native to Madagascar.
- The smallest lemur is the Madame Berthe's mouse lemur, which weighs only 30 grams.
- Lemurs have a highly developed sense of smell, and some species use scent to mark their territory.
- Lemurs have specially adapted feet which enable them to grasp branches and tree trunks.
- Ring-tailed lemurs have a distinctive black-and-white striped tail that can be used to express their emotions.

- Lemurs are omnivores, with a varied diet that includes fruits, leaves, insects and even small vertebrates.
- Lemurs are seasonal breeders, with mating season typically occurring during the wet season.
- Some lemur species are active during the day, while others are active at night.
- Lemurs communicate through vocalizations and body language.
- Lemurs can be found in a variety of habitats, from forests to grassy areas.
- Lemurs are social creatures, living in groups of five to thirty individuals.
- Lemurs have a fused digit on their hands and feet, allowing them to grip objects more effectively.
- Lemurs have a special adaptation which allows them to leap up to 15 meters between tree branches.
- Lemurs are threatened by habitat destruction, hunting, and the illegal pet trade.
- The aye-aye is a rare nocturnal lemur that feeds on insects and fruit.

LIONS

LIONS ARE one of the most majestic creatures on Earth and are known for their strength and power. Amazingly, these powerful cats are able to run at speeds of up to 81 kilometers per hour and leap up to 3 meters in one bound! Here are some more amazing facts about lions:

- Lions are the only cats that live in groups, called prides.
- A male lion's mane can increase in size when he is stressed or angry.
- Lions are born with blue eyes, which change to the golden color they are known for as they grow older.
- Female lions do the majority of the hunting in a pride.
- Lions are the second largest cats in the world after tigers.
- Lions can sleep up to 20 hours a day.
- Lions can live up to 14 years in the wild, and up to 20 years in captivity.
- A lion's roar can be heard up to 8 kilometers away.
- The average weight of a male lion is 190 kilograms.

- Lions are the only cats that have a tuft of fur at the end of their tail.
- Lions are able to see six times better than humans in low light.
- The average lifespan of a lion in the wild is around 8 to 10 years.
- The closest living relatives of lions are tigers, cheetahs, and leopards.

LIZARDS

LIZARDS ARE fascinating creatures with a plethora of incredible abilities. From many species being able to shed their tails to regrow them to others being able to run across water, there are many incredible facts about lizards.

- Many species of lizards have the ability to change their color over time.
- Some lizards have the ability to regenerate lost limbs.
- Some species of lizards can change genders.
- Some species of lizards have the ability to produce venom.
- Some species of lizards can "freeze" or suspend themselves in a state of immobility for long periods of time.
- Some species of lizards can climb walls and even walk on ceilings.
- Some lizards have the ability to burrow underground to escape predators.
- Some species of lizards can climb trees and glide from tree to tree.

- Some species of lizards can survive in extremely hot and cold temperatures.
- Some species of lizards can breathe through their skin.
- Some species of lizards can sleep while standing up.
- Some species of lizards lay eggs, while others are live-bearing.
- Some species of lizards can change the size of their eyes in response to different levels of light.

INTERLUDE: ANIMAL HOMES

Animal homes are incredibly complex and diverse. From underground tunnels to towering trees and intricate networks of webs, each animal species has developed its own unique way of keeping safe and warm. Here are some amazing facts about animal homes:

- The arctic fox builds large, complex dens underground to protect itself from the cold winter temperatures.
- The kangaroo rat builds its nests by digging burrows and lining them with plant materials.
- The African bullfrog builds a unique 'bubble' home by forming a thin layer of mud on top of a still pond, which provides shelter and protection from predators.

- The kingfisher builds its nest in narrow crevices in the banks of rivers, ponds and lakes.
- The bowerbird collects sticks and other objects to build an elaborate structure called a bower, in order to attract a mate.
- The armadillo digs extensive network of burrows that can reach over 20 metres in length and can be used by other animals as a source of shelter.
- The barn owl builds nests in tree cavities and abandoned buildings, and can reach speeds of up to 60 mph while in flight.
- The silkworm spins a silken cocoon around itself to form a protective sheath.
- The elephant builds a temporary home called a 'midden', which is made up of branches, leaves and mud.
- The shovel-nosed snake digs a shallow burrow in the sand which it uses for protection from predators.
- The bumblebee builds its nest in underground cavities, such as abandoned mouse burrows, and guards it fiercely.
- The flamingo builds a cone-shaped nest out of mud and twigs and lines it with secreted saliva.
- The swift builds a cup-shaped nest on the walls of cliffs and buildings, and can fly over 100 mph.

MONKEYS

MONKEYS ARE INCREDIBLY intelligent and fascinating animals. They have the ability to learn complex tasks and communicate with each other using a variety of vocalizations, gestures, and facial expressions. They are highly social and can form close bonds with one another, as well as with humans. Here are some amazing facts about monkeys:

- Monkeys have the ability to use tools and even manipulate certain objects.
- Monkeys have personalities and can display a range of emotions.
- They can recognize themselves in a mirror, which is a skill that few animals have.
- Monkeys have an impressive memory and can remember the face of someone they have seen before.
- Most monkeys are able to swim and dive underwater.
- Some species of monkeys have prehensile tails, which can be used to grip objects.

- They have opposable thumbs which help them to grasp things.
- Monkeys can live in a wide range of habitats, from tropical rainforests to deserts.
- Most species of monkeys can live for up to 25 years.
- They have highly developed senses of sight, smell and hearing.
- Monkeys are omnivores and can eat both plants and animals.
- They have an excellent sense of balance and can leap long distances.
- Monkeys have advanced problem solving skills which they use to find food and survive in their environments.

MICE

MICE ARE INCREDIBLY FASCINATING CREATURES, with some amazing capabilities. They are among the most intelligent rodents, able to learn and remember complex tasks, and have an impressive ability to problem solve. They are also incredibly fast, and can run up to 8 miles per hour, as well as jump up to a foot in the air.

- Mice have an incredibly acute sense of hearing, able to detect noises at frequencies up to 80 kHz.
- Mice are highly social animals, living in large groups and forming strong bonds with each other.
- Mice have an impressive ability to solve complex problems.
- Mice can identify familiar individuals through their urine.
- Mice have an excellent sense of smell, able to detect odors up to 10,000 times better than humans.
- Mice have excellent memory and can remember tasks up to 3 months after completing them.
- Mice can detect a single particle of food up to 5 inches away.

- Mice are incredibly agile, able to squeeze through tiny gaps and climb vertical walls.
- Mice are nocturnal animals, meaning they are active at night and sleep during the day.
- Mice have poor vision, but can detect movement up to 15 feet away.
- Mice have a unique eye structure, with a large lens, short eyeball, and a wide field of vision.
- Mice can swim up to half a mile and can tread water for up to three days.
- Mice are sensitive to ultrasonic frequencies, enabling them to detect sounds beyond the human range.
- Mice use their whiskers to navigate in the dark and detect changes in air currents.

OCTOPUSES

OCTOPUSES ARE some of the most fascinating creatures in the ocean. Their complex nervous systems and sophisticated camouflage techniques have earned them a reputation as masters of disguise and one of the most intelligent invertebrates. Here are some amazing facts about octopuses:

- Octopuses have three hearts.
- An octopus can squeeze its entire body through an opening the size of a quarter.
- Octopuses can learn to solve puzzles and recognize human faces.
- Octopuses have blue blood thanks to their copper-rich hemocyanin.
- Octopuses can rapidly change colors and even their textures to blend into their surroundings.
- Octopus skin is covered in photophores, allowing them to communicate with light.
- Octopuses can jet through the water by shooting a stream of water out of their mantles.
- Octopuses have a well-developed sense of touch, allowing them to identify objects in the dark.

- Octopuses have suction cups on their tentacles that can detect pressure, taste, and smell.
- Octopuses can regrow arms that have been lost or damaged.
- Octopuses can change the shape and texture of their bodies to mimic other sea creatures.
- Octopuses are cannibals and will eat other octopuses.
- Octopuses have the ability to regenerate neurons and heal after a traumatic injury.
- Octopuses have the ability to regenerate their inner organs.
- Octopuses typically have a lifespan of up to 5 years, although some species can live much longer.

OPOSSUMS

OPOSSUMS ARE AMAZING CREATURES. They are the only marsupial native to North America, and have a remarkable ability to eat almost anything and survive many different environments. They are also incredibly intelligent, have an impressive disease-fighting immune system, and are incredibly agile climbers. Here are some amazing facts about opossums:

- Opossums have 50 teeth, which is more than any other mammal in North America.
- They have the ability to go into a catatonic state, which is commonly referred to as "playing possum".
- Opossums are immune to most snake venom.
- They are very clean animals and groom themselves regularly, like cats.
- Opossums are excellent swimmers and can also hold their breath underwater for up to five minutes.
- They have a very strong sense of smell, up to 50 times greater than that of a dog.
- The majority of opossum diet consists of insects, slugs, snails, rodents, and carrion.

- Opossums can use their opposable thumbs to open doors, drawers, and latches.
- Opossums can give birth to up to 13 young in one litter.
- They can carry up to 7 babies on their back at once.
- Opossums will often play dead when threatened by a predator, entering into a catatonic state for up to 4 hours.
- Opossums have a prehensile tail which can be used to grab branches and helps them climb.
- One full opossum can eat up to 4,000 ticks in a single season.
- A group of opossums is called a passel or a yeard.
- Their life span in the wild is typically 2-4 years.

ORANG-UTANS

ORANG-UTANS ARE FASCINATING CREATURES, with many amazing facts about them. From their remarkable intelligence to their lanky limbs and shaggy coats, there are so many incredible things to learn about these gentle giants. Here are some amazing facts about orang-utans:

- Orang-utans are one of the two species of great apes native to Asia, the other being the Gibbon.
- Adult orang-utans can weigh up to 200 lbs.
- Orang-utans have long arms and exceptionally long hands and fingers, which they use to move through the trees.
- Orang-utans are the most solitary of the great apes, with adult males and females living separately.
- Orang-utans are highly intelligent and can make and use tools.
- Orang-utans have the longest childhood dependence of any animal, with young remaining with their mothers for up to 8 years.

- Orang-utans have a special relationship with their mothers, with the mother teaching them important survival skills.
- Orang-utans communicate through facial expressions and vocalisations.
- Orang-utans are mainly frugivorous, with fruit forming the majority of their diet.
- Orang-utans have an impressive sense of smell, which they use to find fruit and to identify potential mates.
- Orang-utans are the most arboreal of the great apes, spending most of their time in trees.
- Orang-utans have an incredibly long lifespan, living up to 45 years in the wild and over 60 years in captivity.
- Orang-utans are one of the most endangered species of great ape, with their population declining rapidly due to habitat loss, illegal pet trade, and poaching.
- Orang-utans are the only non-human species known to use leaves to make rain hats.
- Orang-utans are incredibly strong, able to carry up to five times their own body weight.

OSTRICHES

OSTRICHES ARE the world's largest and heaviest birds and are truly amazing creatures. They have powerful, long legs which enable them to run up to 40 mph and can sprint up to 70 mph, making them the fastest land birds. They are also the only birds which can survive without drinking water, as they get all the moisture they need from the plants they eat. Here are some amazing facts about ostriches:

- Ostriches have the largest eyes of any land animal.
- An ostrich egg is the largest of any bird species, and can weigh up to 1.4kg (3 lbs).
- Ostriches can live up to 75 years in the wild.
- Ostriches can cover up to 3.2m (10ft) in one stride.
- An ostrich's kick is powerful enough to kill a lion.
- Ostriches can go for weeks without drinking water.
- They lay the largest eggs of any bird in the world.
- Ostriches are omnivorous and eat both plants and insects.
- Ostriches have the strongest legs of any bird, enabling them to jump up to 2.1m (7ft) off the ground.

- Ostriches make a wide variety of sounds including hissing, grunting and booming.
- Ostriches can live in temperatures ranging from -40°C to 40°C.
- Ostriches have excellent eyesight and are able to see predators from a distance.
- Ostriches are able to fly short distances – up to 10 metres.
- The wingspan of an adult ostrich is about 2 metres.

OTTERS

OTTERS ARE INCREDIBLY interesting and unique animals. They are one of the few mammals that use tools, have a complex social structure, and can live both in the water and on land. Here are some amazing facts about otters:

- Otters have webbed feet, allowing them to swim up to 6 miles per hour and dive up to 300 feet.
- Otters have the densest fur of any mammal, with over one million hairs per square inch.
- Otters are able to turn their eyes and ears underwater in order to search for prey.
- Otters have a distinctive whistle that they use to communicate with each other.
- Otters use stones as tools to open mollusks and clams.
- Otters wrap themselves in kelp underwater to keep from floating away when they sleep.
- Otters can live up to 20 years in the wild.
- The smallest of the otter species is the Asian small-clawed otter, which can grow to be about two feet long and weigh 8 lbs.

- The largest of the otter species is the giant otter, which can grow to be up to seven feet long and weigh up to 70 lbs.
- The youngest otter can swim within hours of being born and can dive within days.
- Otters are incredibly playful and can often be found sliding down banks, chasing after each other, and playing catch with rocks and sticks.
- Otters are members of the weasel family and are closely related to ferrets and badgers.
- Otters can close their nostrils and ears when they are underwater.
- Otters are top predators and eat a variety of fish, crabs, and other small animals.
- Otters have a special pouch in their cheeks that they use to carry food to their young.

OWLS

OWLS ARE some of the most fascinating creatures of the avian world. They possess incredible adaptations and are renowned for their excellent vision and hearing. Their wings are designed for silent flight, and their feathers are specially adapted to help them fly with barely any sound. Here are some amazing facts about owls:

- Owls have asymmetrical ears, which helps them more accurately pinpoint the location of their prey.
- Most owls are nocturnal, meaning they are active during the night.
- Owls may look cuddly, but they have razor-sharp talons and beaks for catching their prey.
- Owls can turn their necks up to 270 degrees in either direction.
- Owls can hear much better than humans, and they can detect sounds up to four times farther away.
- Owls don't build nests, but they do use nests made by other animals.
- Owls have unique feathers that minimize turbulence and noise when they fly.

- Owls can see in the dark, thanks to their large, forward-facing eyes.
- The northern spotted owl is a threatened species in the United States.
- The biggest owl in the world is the Eurasian eagle-owl, which has a wingspan of up to 6.6 feet.
- The smallest owl in the world is the elf owl, which is only about 5 inches tall.
- The eyes of an owl are not true "eyeballs." They are elongated tubes, which gives them their large eyes and wide field of view.
- The facial disc of an owl helps them to funnel sound to their ears.
- Owls have three eyelids: one for blinking, one for sleeping, and one for keeping the eye clean and healthy.

PANDAS

PANDAS ARE TRULY INCREDIBLE ANIMALS. Not only are they captivating to look at, but they are also incredibly intelligent and strong. They are unique among bears in that they have an extra bone in their wrist which helps them to better grip objects such as bamboo stalks. Here are some amazing facts about pandas:

- Pandas can eat up to 20kg of bamboo a day.
- They have been known to climb as high as 13,000 feet to feed on higher-growing bamboo.
- A panda can live up to 20 years in the wild.
- They have an amazing ability to remember where they have found food before.
- Pandas use vocalizations, scent marking, and even handstands to communicate and mark their territory.
- Pandas are one of the only carnivorous mammals to have evolved to be exclusively vegetarian.
- At birth, the cubs are blind and helpless, measuring only 15 cm (6 in) and weighing less than 150 grams (0.33 pounds).

- Despite their cumbersome shape, pandas can run, climb trees, and swim.
- In the wild, pandas primarily feed on bamboo, but in captivity, they also eat apples, bananas, fish, eggs, and yams.
- Pandas are excellent swimmers, having webbed feet and a powerful tail to help them steer.
- Pandas have a special pouch in their cheeks to store food while they are eating.
- Pandas have an incredibly strong jaw and can crush bamboo stems that are up to 5 cm (2 in) thick.
- Pandas have a very slow reproductive rate, with females typically bearing one cub every two years.

PARROTS AND MACAWS

PARROTS AND MACAWS are two of the most beautiful and intelligent bird species in the world, capable of imitating human speech and understanding complex commands. Here are some fascinating facts about them.

- There are over 350 species of parrots and macaws.
- Parrots and macaws have strong, curved beaks which they use to crack open nuts and other hard-shelled fruits.
- Parrots and macaws have a life expectancy of anywhere between 15 and 100 years.
- The longest recorded flight of a parrot or macaw was 7,500 miles.
- The hyacinth macaw is the largest parrot species, with a wingspan of up to 1.3m.
- The smallest parrot species is the pygmy parrot, with a length of only 6cm.
- Macaws and parrots have strong, curved claws which they use to climb and hang from branches.

- Some parrots, such as the grey parrot and the kea, are known for their intelligence and can be taught to imitate human speech.
- The blue-and-yellow macaw has a diet mainly consisting of nuts, fruits and vegetables.
- The red-and-green macaw has a diet mainly consisting of insects and carrion.
- The palm cockatoo is the only parrot species that builds its own nest.
- The kakapo is the only parrot species that is flightless.
- The black palm cockatoo is the only parrot species that uses tools to forage for food.
- The hoatzin is the only parrot species that can digest its own food by fermenting it in its crop.
- The yellow-headed amazon is the only parrot species known to use tools to make its nests.

PEACOCKS

PEACOCKS ARE AN AMAZING BIRD SPECIES, boasting an array of impressive features. Their vibrant colors, long tail feathers, and eye-catching courtship displays make them one of the most iconic and strikingly beautiful birds in the world.

- Peacocks can reach up to 6 feet in height and weigh 8-13 lbs.
- Peacocks are native to India and Sri Lanka and are kept as ornamental birds all over the world.
- The males are the ones with the colorful plumage, while the females are typically duller and smaller.
- The eye-like spots on the peacock's tail are called ocelli.
- A peacock's train contains up to 200 feathers and can be up to 200 centimeters long.
- Peacocks can fly, but they prefer to walk.
- Peacocks are omnivores, meaning they eat both plants and small animals.
- Peacocks can live up to 20 years in the wild.

- Peacocks can make a variety of sounds, including loud shrieks and cackles.
- The male peacock's courtship display involves fanning out his tail feathers, shaking his head, and making loud calls.
- Peacocks are social birds and live in large groups called parties.
- The peacock's impressive colors are created by specialized cells in the feathers called melanin.
- Peacocks are polygamous, meaning they mate with multiple partners.
- Peacock feathers are believed to bring good luck in some cultures.
- Peacocks are related to pheasants and chickens.

PELICANS

PELICANS ARE INCREDIBLE BIRDS, highly adapted for life on the water. They have a large pouch on their throat which is used to scoop up fish, and their wingspan can reach up to 9 feet! Here are some amazing facts about pelicans:

- Pelicans can fly up to 50 miles per hour.
- Pelicans can dive underwater to depths of up to 16 feet.
- Pelicans can drink sea water by using special glands to expel the salt.
- Pelicans use their webbed feet to help them swim.
- Pelicans can stay in the air for up to 24 hours.
- Pelicans can store up to 3 gallons of water in their throat pouch.
- Pelicans have about 30 feathers in the front of their pouch for filtering food.
- Pelicans have one of the longest bills of any bird species, measuring up to 18 inches.
- Pelicans can be found in all continents except Antarctica.

- The oldest known wild pelican lived to be 27 years old.
- Pelicans can sleep in the air by folding their wings and gliding.
- Pelicans use their large bills to battle each other for mates during mating season.
- Pelicans can see well both in the air and underwater.
- Pelicans can eat up to 4 pounds of fish per day.
- Pelicans are considered a symbol of peace and prosperity in some cultures.

PENGUINS

PENGUINS ARE a species of flightless birds that live primarily in the Southern Hemisphere. They are incredibly adapted to the cold and have some extraordinary features that make them unique among birds. Here are some amazing facts about penguins:

- Penguins are able to drink salt water by filtering it through their specialized glands.
- Penguins use their wings to "fly" through the water at speeds up to 15 miles per hour.
- Penguins are able to dive deeper than any other bird, reaching depths up to 1,800 feet.
- Penguins have an extra layer of insulating fat that keeps them warm even in the coldest temperatures.
- Penguins have special flaps of skin that allow them to close off their nostrils while they are underwater.
- Penguins molt, or shed their feathers, every year.
- Penguins are some of the longest living birds in the world, with lifespans of up to 25 years.
- Penguins are social creatures and form strong family bonds with their partners and chicks.

- Penguins perform intricate courtship rituals to attract their mates.
- Penguins care for their young and help to keep them safe and warm.
- Penguins even have their own language.
- Penguins have a unique way of walking on land, called a "tobogganing" gait.
- Penguins use their beaks to find food by sensing the vibrations of their prey.
- Penguins have excellent eyesight both on land and underwater.
- Penguins have an impressive memory, able to remember their individual feeding grounds and other locations.

PIGS

PIGS ARE INCREDIBLY intelligent and inquisitive animals, with a strong sense of social structure. They are highly adaptable and can live in almost any environment, from desert heat to snowy winters. Pigs have extraordinary senses, with an acute sense of smell and good hearing. Their eyesight is not as good as other animals, however they rely on their other senses to navigate and survive in their habitats. Here are some more amazing facts about pigs:

- A pig's snout is an important tool they use to dig and find food.
- Pigs communicate with each other through grunts and squeals.
- Pigs can run at speeds of up to 11 miles per hour.
- Pigs are omnivores, meaning they eat both plants and animals.
- Pigs can recognize and remember other pigs, even after being separated for long periods of time.
- Pigs are very clean animals who keep their living space tidy.

- Pigs can learn how to perform simple tasks after just a few repetitions.
- Pigs possess corkscrew shaped, chisel-like teeth which never stop growing.
- Pigs can sleep for up to 8 hours a day.
- Pigs are highly social animals, living in groups called sounders.
- Pigs are very good swimmers, able to stay afloat for up to 5 hours at a time.
- Pigs can enjoy music, often nodding their heads and swaying their bodies to the beat.
- Pigs are one of the smartest animals, ranking fourth in intelligence behind chimpanzees, dolphins, and elephants.
- Pigs have unique fingerprint-like patterns on their snouts, which can be used to tell them apart.
- Pigs have an excellent sense of direction and can easily find their way home from distances of up to 12 miles.

PIGEONS

PIGEONS ARE TRULY REMARKABLE BIRDS. Their incredible navigation ability allows them to travel long distances and find their way back home. They have amazing eyesight and can recognize people from far away. They can even distinguish between shapes, colors, and patterns. Impressive! Here are some amazing facts about pigeons:

- Pigeons can see ultraviolet light, which is invisible to humans.
- Pigeons can remember up to 200 individuals within their flock.
- Pigeons can fly up to top speeds of 75 mph.
- Pigeons are able to identify their eggs and chicks despite the fact that they look very similar.
- Pigeons can fly up to 600 miles in a single day.
- Pigeons have demonstrated the ability to solve complex problems in captivity.
- Pigeons have an excellent sense of direction and can find their way home from hundreds of miles away.

- Scientists have demonstrated that pigeons can differentiate between written words and handwritten characters.
- Pigeons can recognize their own reflections in a mirror.
- Pigeons are capable of understanding symbols and can be trained to distinguish between individual letters of the alphabet.
- Pigeons can learn to recognize different types of music.
- Pigeons can recognize individual people from a distance.
- Pigeons can remember their route home even when flying in unfamiliar territory.
- Pigeons have an advanced sense of smell and can detect food from hundreds of feet away.

POLAR BEARS

SEE ALSO: BEARS

POLAR BEARS ARE among the strongest, largest, and most powerful of all bears, making them a formidable species. They are amazing animals with a variety of unique adaptations which help them to survive in their icy habitats. Here are some amazing facts about polar bears:

- They are the the world's largest land predators.
- Polar bears are great swimmers, able to swim up to 6 miles per hour.
- Their fur is not white; it's actually transparent.
- They have a keen sense of smell, allowing them to detect prey up to a mile away.
- Polar bears have a thick layer of blubber, protecting them from the cold.
- They can live up to 25 years in the wild.
- Polar bears are considered marine mammals since they spend a lot of time in the water.
- Their paws are very wide, helping them to walk on the snow and ice.
- They can go up to two months without eating.

- They can consume up to 15% of their body weight in a single meal.
- Polar bears are mainly carnivores, relying mostly on seal meat for their diet.
- They have the ability to fast for up to eight months each year.
- The scientific name for polar bears is Ursus maritimus, which means sea bear.
- Cubs are born blind and only open their eyes after 10 days.

PORCUPINES

PORCUPINES ARE FASCINATING CREATURES! With over 30 species, they are the second largest group of rodents in the world. They have a unique ability to defend themselves with their quills. Porcupines are also quite long-lived, with some living up to 20 years in the wild. Amazing facts about porcupines:

- Porcupines have an impressive coat of 30,000 quills which can be up to 10 inches long.
- Porcupines have razor-sharp teeth, which they use to chew on wood and bark to get their nutritional needs.
- Porcupines are excellent swimmers and can stay submerged in water for up to five minutes.
- Porcupines are active during the night, and can spend up to 15 hours foraging for food.
- Porcupines are herbivores and their diet consists mainly of roots, bark, fruits, and vegetables.
- Porcupines can make a variety of noises such as grunts, squeals and hisses to communicate.

- Porcupines are solitary creatures and mark their territory with scent glands located on their back and feet.
- Porcupines have a great sense of smell, which helps them find food in the dark.
- Porcupines are excellent climbers and can use their quills to grasp onto tree trunks and branches. They have a prehensile tail which they use to help balance while they climb trees.
- Porcupines have very poor eyesight, relying mostly on their sense of smell and hearing to detect predators.
- Porcupines are found in many parts of the world, including North and South America, Asia, and Africa.
- Porcupines usually have one offspring at a time, but can have up to three litters in one year.
- Porcupines have a unique ability to shed their quills when threatened, which can be replaced in as little as two months.
- Porcupines are considered a pest by farmers and gardeners as they can cause significant damage to crops and trees.

PRAYING MANTISES

PRAYING mantises are truly remarkable creatures. These insects are capable of camouflage, camouflage to the point of disappearing against the background and ambushing prey. They have large eyes which give them excellent vision and they can even rotate their head 180 degrees to get an even better view of their surroundings. They are also capable of eating a wide variety of prey and they have even been known to eat small birds on occasion. Here's a list of some amazing facts about praying mantises:

- Praying mantises can live up to a year in the wild.
- Praying mantises are ambush predators, with their camouflage allowing them to blend in with their surroundings and surprise their prey.
- The male praying mantis is usually smaller than the female and is often eaten by the female after mating.
- Praying mantises are capable of leaping up to several times their own body length.
- Praying mantises have triangular heads with two large compound eyes, as well as three smaller eyes located between them.

- Praying mantises are capable of complex behaviors, such as stalking and capturing prey.
- Praying mantises have five sets of spines on their forelegs which are used to capture prey.
- Praying mantises can fly, although they are not strong fliers.
- Praying mantises can eat a wide variety of prey, including small insects, spiders, and even small birds.
- Praying mantises can also feed on nectar, pollen, and fruits.
- Praying mantises possess a unique reproductive strategy known as "sexual cannibalism".
- Praying mantises can go through a process of "molting", where they shed their skin and grow larger.
- Praying mantises are found on every continent except Antarctica.
- Praying mantises are considered a keystone species, meaning that their presence is beneficial in maintaining a healthy ecosystem.

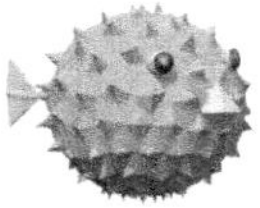

PUFFERFISH

PUFFERFISH ARE INCREDIBLE CREATURES, capable of swallowing large amounts of water and inflating their bodies to several times their normal size. They also have very strong toxins in their skin and organs, which can be lethal to other fish, and even humans.

- Some pufferfish can grow up to 80 cm long.
- Many pufferfish produce a toxin called tetrodotoxin, which can be lethal to humans.
- The spines of pufferfish are covered in a thin layer of slime, which helps them to move through the water.
- Pufferfish use their pectoral fins to steer, while their tail helps them to move forward.
- When threatened, some pufferfish will make a loud buzzing noise by vibrating their swim bladder.
- The blowfish uses its inflated body to scare off predators. A pufferfish can make itself almost spherical by swallowing water or air.
- Pufferfish have a very slow metabolism, and can go without food for long periods of time.
- Some species of pufferfish can live up to 30 years.

- Pufferfish are highly intelligent, and can learn to recognize their owners.
- Pufferfish use their teeth to scrape algae off rocks and coral.
- The skin of a pufferfish is covered with small spikes, which are used for protection.
- Some species of pufferfish can change color in order to blend in with their environment.
- Pufferfish have an extendable stomach, which can stretch to accommodate large meals.
- Pufferfish eggs are covered in a hard shell, which helps to protect them from predators.

RABBITS

RABBITS ARE incredible animals known for their furry coats, big ears, and fluffy tails. They are also incredibly intelligent and have a number of unique behaviors and adaptations which make them one of the most interesting creatures on the planet. Here are some amazing facts about rabbits:

- Rabbits can see in almost 360 degrees.
- Rabbits are naturally clean animals and keep their fur groomed and free of debris.
- A group of rabbits is called a 'warren'.
- Rabbits are able to jump up to three feet in the air.
- Rabbits have over two hundred million scent cells, making them excellent smellers.
- Rabbit teeth never stop growing.
- Rabbits can run up to 25 miles per hour.
- Rabbits have a special digestive system which allows them to re-ingest their own soft feces for extra nutrition.
- Rabbits can live up to 10 years in the wild and 10-12 years in captivity.

- Rabbits can eat their own food twice, digesting it differently each time.
- Rabbits are born blind and without fur.
- Rabbits are social animals and enjoy interacting with other rabbits and humans.
- Rabbits can produce 20-50 droppings in a single day.
- Rabbits can hear both high and low frequency sounds.
- Rabbits are born with open eyes, unlike other baby mammals.

RACCOONS

RACCOONS ARE A HIGHLY intelligent species of mammal, known for their distinctive black mask and bandit-like behavior. They are skilled climbers, swimmers and problem solvers, and are even capable of learning how to open complex locks. Here are some amazing facts about raccoons:

- Raccoons can run up to 15 miles per hour.
- They are nocturnal animals and can often be found foraging for food at night.
- Raccoons are omnivores and will eat nearly anything, from insects to fruits and vegetables.
- They have very dexterous front paws, which allow them to open containers, untie knots, and even use tools.
- Raccoons can live up to 16 years in the wild.
- They have excellent vision and a keen sense of hearing, which helps them detect prey.
- Raccoons have a highly developed sense of touch, allowing them to identify objects in complete darkness.

- They are capable of swimming in both fresh and salt water.
- Raccoons have a special fur that helps insulate them from cold weather and also repels water.
- They are found on every continent except Antarctica.
- Raccoons are very social animals and often live in large groups.
- Females have been known to teach their young how to forage for food.
- They have excellent memories and can remember solutions to problems for up to three years.
- Raccoons are capable of purring, chirping and whistling to communicate with each other.
- They can recognize their own reflections in mirrors.

RATS

RATS ARE INCREDIBLY INTELLIGENT ANIMALS, with the capacity to learn complex behaviors and solve problems. They can even recognize faces and remember the emotions associated with them. Rats are also incredibly social, forming strong family and social bonds with other rats. Furthermore, these animals have impressive metabolisms, allowing them to withstand extreme temperatures and remain healthy.

- Rats have an excellent sense of smell and can navigate their way through a maze using scent.
- Rats can learn to recognize and respond to different sounds.
- Rats have excellent memories, capable of remembering events and emotions associated with them.
- Rats have the ability to learn complex behaviors and solve problems.
- Rats have an impressive metabolism, helping them to maintain their health even in extreme temperatures.

- Rats can taste sweet, salty, sour and bitter flavors.
- Rats are able to pick up objects with their tails.
- Rats are highly intelligent, capable of making decisions and problem solving.
- Rats can survive falls from high heights because of the structure of their skeletal system.
- Rats can sense electrical and magnetic fields, allowing them to detect changes in the environment.
- Rats are incredibly agile and can jump up to three feet in the air.
- Rats have an excellent sense of hearing, capable of hearing ultrasonic noises.
- Rats have an acute sense of touch, sensitive enough to detect small changes in air pressure.
- Rats can swim for up to three days without stopping.

RAVENS

SEE ALSO: CROWS

RAVENS ARE one of the most intelligent birds on Earth, capable of complex problem solving and tool use. Ravens have remarkable memories, able to remember individual human faces for up to five years. They have also been observed playing games with each other for entertainment. Here are some amazing facts about ravens:

- Ravens can recognize themselves in a mirror.
- Ravens can imitate the calls of other species.
- A single raven can be heard up to three miles away.
- Ravens can reach speeds of up to 56 km/h while flying.
- Ravens are omnivorous, eating a wide range of foods from small animals to fruits and nuts.
- Ravens establish lifelong monogamous relationships.
- Ravens have an incredibly broad range of vocalizations, up to 30 different calls.
- Ravens are very social and often travel in large flocks of up to 100 birds.

- Ravens are highly intelligent and able to solve complex problems.
- Ravens can recognize human faces and remember them for up to five years.
- Ravens have been observed using tools to obtain food.
- The average lifespan of a raven is up to 16 years.
- Ravens can travel up to 250 km in a single day.
- Ravens will play games with each other, such as keep away, for fun.
- Ravens are found in all continents except Antarctica.

RAYS

RAYS ARE amazing sea creatures with unique adaptations for their aquatic environment. They have flat bodies, often with wings that resemble those of a bat or kite, and can glide gracefully through the water. Rays can vary greatly in size, from the tiny pygmy wedgefish to the enormous manta ray. Here are some amazing facts about rays:

- Rays can live up to 25 years.
- Some rays can grow up to 7 meters in length.
- The smallest ray is the dwarf electric ray, which reaches up to 8.5 centimeters in length.
- Rays have a cartilaginous skeleton, instead of a bony skeleton.
- Some species of ray can produce an electric shock.
- Rays are generally harmless unless disturbed or threatened.
- Some species of ray can eat prey up to five times their own size.
- A female ray can produce up to four million eggs at once.

- Many rays migrate to shallow waters to feed and reproduce.
- Rays have specially adapted eyes to help them see in murky waters.
- Rays have a unique method of feeding, known as 'suction feeding'.
- They have bellies covered in sandpaper-like skin for protection.
- Rays can make their own sound, or 'buzz', to scare away predators.
- They have a unique 'wing-like' tail that helps them to swim.
- Some species of ray are venomous.

SALMON

SALMON ARE one of the most incredible creatures in the world. They are capable of traveling incredible distances, living in both fresh and saltwater environments. Here are some amazing facts about salmon:

- Salmon can travel thousands of miles in their lifetime and migrate vast distances between fresh and saltwater habitats.
- Salmon are anadromous, meaning they spend part of their lives in freshwater and part of their lives in saltwater.
- Salmon are able to find their way back to the same location to spawn by using their olfactory memory.
- Salmon have the capacity to change the color of their skin, depending on the environment they're in.
- Salmon can grow up to 4 feet in length when they are fully mature.
- Salmon can weigh up to 55 pounds when fully grown.
- Salmon can live up to 8 years in the wild.
- Salmon can jump up to 6 feet in the air.

- The name "salmon" comes from the Latin word "salmo," which means "leaper".
- Wild salmon contain more omega 3 fatty acids than farmed salmon.
- Wild salmon can swim up to 10 miles an hour.
- Salmon are born in freshwater streams and rivers and then migrate to the ocean to feed.
- Salmon are an important part of the food chain, providing a vital food source for larger animals such as bears, eagles, and orcas.
- Salmon have complex sensory organs which allow them to detect chemical signals in their environment.

SCORPIONS

SCORPIONS HAVE SOME AMAZING FEATURES. For example, they can survive up to 6 weeks without food, they can survive up to a year without water, they can live up to 25 years, they are able to survive extreme temperatures, and they can regenerate lost tails. Here are some more amazing facts about scorpions:

- Scorpions are able to detect vibrations and movements with their pincers.
- Scorpions are able to swim and may even be found in the ocean.
- They can change color to blend into their environment.
- Scorpions exhibit fluorescent colors under UV light.
- Scorpions are nocturnal and are active at night.
- They have 8 eyes, but despite this, they have poor vision.
- They can jump up to 2 feet in the air!
- They have an exoskeleton that they shed and replace periodically.

- Scorpions can vary in size from 1/8th of an inch to over 8 inches in length.
- Scorpions can have anywhere up to 120 babies at a time.
- The venom of a scorpion is used in medicinal treatments.
- Scorpions are predators, mainly eating insects and spiders.
- They can move up to 3 feet per second.
- Scorpions are found on all continents except Antarctica.
- The oldest known scorpion fossil dates back to 437 million years ago.

SEA BIRDS

SEA BIRDS ARE HIGHLY remarkable creatures with a number of interesting attributes. They possess the unique ability to swim, take off from the water and fly, are able to fly for long distances, have an impressive adaptation to different environments, and are some of the longest living animals in the world. Here is a list of some amazing facts about sea birds:

- Sea birds have highly waterproof feathers that allow them to stay dry and warm when diving underwater.
- Most sea birds have salt glands located near the eyes and nostrils that help them to excrete excess salt from their bodies.
- Albatrosses have the longest wingspan of any living sea bird, measuring up to 11-12 feet!
- The Arctic tern is one of the longest-distance migrants, travelling from the Arctic to the Antarctic each year.
- Puffins eat fish and small marine animals, storing them in their beak for later consumption.

- Many types of sea birds, such as razorbills, guillemots, and murres, dive deep underwater to hunt for food.
- Albatrosses can spend up to 10 days at sea without ever needing to land.
- The great frigatebird is the only bird known to steal food from other sea birds.
- The wandering albatross can fly up to speeds of almost 100 km/h (62 mph)!
- Some sea birds, such as the wandering albatross, mate for life and can live up to 50 years.
- The kittiwake is a type of gull that builds nests by attaching them to cliff faces.
- Cormorants have specialized feathers that allow them to dive deeper for longer periods of time.
- Penguins are the only sea birds that can't fly but can swim up to speeds of 22 km/h (14 mph).
- Aptenodytes patagonicus (the emperor penguin) is the tallest and heaviest species of sea bird.
- The Atlantic puffin can dive up to 79 metres (260 ft) below the surface in search of food.

SEAHORSES

SEAHORSES ARE a fascinating animal that have captivated the imaginations of humans for centuries. They are renowned for their unusual curved shape and their ability to travel in both directions, up and down. But there is a lot more to seahorses than meets the eye – here are some of their amazing facts:

- Seahorses are monogamous, often staying with the same mate for years.
- They have prehensile tails that can grab onto objects and help them move.
- They can change the color of their skin to blend in with the environment.
- Every species of seahorse has a unique brood pouch size and placement.
- Seahorses can eat up to 3,000 small meals a day.
- Male seahorses are the ones who give birth to the babies.
- Seahorses have no teeth or stomach and use their snouts to suck up food.

- They are able to survive in saltwater and freshwater environments.
- Unlike most fish, seahorses have eyes that move independently.
- They can swim in any direction – forwards, backwards, up and down.
- Seahorses swim in groups and form unique bonds with each other.
- Seahorses are known to perform synchronised dances with their mates.
- They have specialised cells allowing them to absorb oxygen directly from water.
- Their tails are prehensile, allowing them to cling to seaweed or coral.
- They can live up to 8 years in the wild.

INTERLUDE: ANIMAL SENSES

Animals have amazing senses, far superior to our own in some cases. For example, some species of shark can detect electrical signals from prey, while a fly's vision can detect movement that is imperceptible to the human eye. Here are some more amazing facts about animal senses:

- Some species of toads can sense seismic vibrations through the soil.
- Bats use echolocation to navigate their environment and find prey.
- A dog's sense of smell is 1,000 times better than a human's.

- Penguins have an acute sense of hearing, allowing them to locate their prey in dark and murky waters.
- Sharks can detect even the smallest amount of blood in the water from up to a mile away.
- Cats can see in much lower light levels than humans.
- Owls are able to detect the exact location of the prey they're hunting, even in total darkness.
- Some snakes can sense their prey's heat signature, allowing them to find their prey in the dark.
- Bees can see ultraviolet light and are able to detect the presence of flowers from miles away.
- Frogs can detect vibrations in the water from up to three feet away.
- Some species of fish can detect electrical fields in the water.
- Dolphins use sound waves to create a three-dimensional image of their surroundings.
- Dogs can detect changes in barometric pressure, which can alert them to an approaching storm.
- Some species of ants can detect the Earth's magnetic field to help them find their way home.
- Salmon can detect the presence of predators from over a mile away.

SEALS AND SEALIONS

SEALS AND SEALIONS are fascinating creatures of the sea, with some incredible adaptations and behaviors. From their ability to dive deeply, to their unique vocalizations, these animals are truly remarkable. Here are some amazing facts about seals and sealions:

- Seals can stay underwater for up to an hour.
- Seals have powerful front flippers that can propel them through the water.
- They have a layer of blubber which helps to insulate them and keep them warm in cold water.
- Seals can reach speeds of up to 25 mph when they are swimming.
- They have a visual range of up to eight times that of humans.
- They have an excellent sense of smell and can detect prey from a long distance.
- Seals have ears which are well adapted to underwater environments and can detect low frequency sound waves.

- Seals can sleep underwater for up to 15 minutes at a time.
- They have a unique vocalization created by vibrations in the larynx.
- Sealions are the only species of seal that can walk on land.
- Sealions can stay underwater for up to 15 minutes.
- Sealions have excellent hearing and can pick up underwater sounds up to two miles away.
- Sealions can use their front flippers to help them move on land.
- Sealions have a thick fur coat to help keep them warm on land and in cold water.
- Sealions can use their tail to help them steer and turn in the water.

SHARKS

SHARKS ARE some of the most mysterious and awe-inspiring creatures in the ocean. These amazing animals have some truly unique characteristics and adaptations that make them stand out from the rest of the oceanic population. Here are some amazing facts about sharks:

- Sharks have been around for over 400 million years, predating even dinosaurs.
- Sharks have extraordinary senses, which allow them to detect electrical signals and pressure changes in the water.
- Sharks can grow up to 41 feet long, making them some of the largest fish in the ocean.
- The smallest shark species, the spined pygmy shark, grows no larger than 8 inches in length.
- Sharks can have up to 3000 teeth in their lifetime.
- Sharks have no bones, their skeletal structure is made up of cartilage.
- They have 6-7 gill slits, instead of the usual one or two.
- Sharks can swim up to 40 miles per hour.

- Sharks can detect a single drop of blood in 25 gallons of water.
- They can sense the Earth's magnetic field, helping them to navigate their way around.
- Sharks do not have a single or a pair of lungs, like other fish, they have a set of 5 to 7 gill arches.
- Most sharks are ovoviviparous, which means they give birth to live young.
- The oldest known shark fossil is over 420 million years old.
- Sharks can often live up to 20 years or more in the wild.
- Some sharks can go into a hibernation-like state called 'tonic immobility'.

SHEEP

SHEEP ARE AMAZING ANIMALS! They have been domesticated for thousands of years and provide us with wool, meat, and milk. They are also surprisingly intelligent animals. Here are some amazing facts about sheep:

- Sheep produce four types of wool: longwool, mediumwool, carpetwool, and lustrewool.
- A single sheep can produce eight to ten pounds of wool per year.
- Sheep have excellent memories, and can remember those they have met before.
- Sheep can recognize one another by their face, just like we recognize friends and family.
- Sheep have very strong maternal instincts and mother sheep can recognize their lambs by their call.
- A newborn lamb can walk within an hour of its birth.
- Sheep have rectangular pupils, which helps them to take in more light and grass when grazing.
- Sheep can reach speeds of up to 40 mph.

- Sheep have a three-chambered stomach for digestion.
- A single sheep can have up to 36 different calls.
- Sheep have split hooves, which helps them to keep their balance on uneven terrain.
- Sheep are most active at dusk and dawn.
- Sheep have excellent eyesight, and can see in color.
- Sheep can also detect movements up to a mile away.
- Sheep are very social animals and prefer to stay in groups.

SKUNKS

SKUNKS ARE AMAZING ANIMALS, capable of a variety of unique behaviors and abilities. They have a remarkable sense of smell and many species are able to spray a powerful odor when threatened. Here are some amazing facts about skunks:

- Skunks have the ability to spray their predators from up to 10 feet away.
- Skunks have an excellent sense of smell, up to 100 times better than a human's.
- They can run up to 15 mph and can swim to escape predators.
- Some skunks have black fur with white stripes, while others may have white fur with black stripes.
- Skunks can live up to 5 years in the wild and up to 10 years in captivity.
- They can spray their predators multiple times in quick succession.
- Skunks are omnivorous and enjoy eating insects, berries, nuts, and carrion.

- They have poor eyesight and rely mostly on their sense of smell and hearing to detect danger.
- Skunks are solitary animals, except during mating season and when raising young.
- They are mostly nocturnal, meaning they are most active at night.
- Skunks have the ability to spray their predators in multiple directions simultaneously. They can also accurately spray the same area multiple times without reloading.
- Skunks are capable of producing different odors depending on the situation.
- They dig burrows, typically in wooded areas, to provide shelter and safety.
- Skunks are non-aggressive and will only spray if they feel threatened or cornered.

SLOTHS

SLOTHS ARE AMAZING ANIMALS! Their slow-moving lifestyle and funny features make them one of the most beloved creatures in the animal kingdom. But there's a lot more to these fascinating creatures than meets the eye. Here are some amazing facts about sloths:

- Sloths can turn their heads 270 degrees.
- Sloths have three stomachs.
- Sloths can swim!
- They have a very low metabolic rate, which allows them to survive on little food.
- Sloths tend to defecate at the same spot in the trees once a week.
- Sloths are amazing climbers and can hang from branches for hours.
- Sloths can live up to 40 years in the wild.
- Their fur is home to many species of moths, beetles, and cockroaches.
- Sloths are nocturnal animals.
- They have long, curved claws to help them cling to branches.

- Sloths have an excellent sense of smell.
- They have an average body temperature of 32 degrees Celsius.
- Sloths have a slow growth rate and take one year to reach adulthood.
- Sloths sleep for 15 to 20 hours a day.
- Sloths have a four-toed front foot and a three-toed back foot.

SNAILS AND SLUGS

SNAILS AND SLUGS have unique characteristics that make them amazing creatures. Here are some amazing facts about snails and slugs:

- Snails and slugs are hermaphroditic, capable of self-fertilization.
- They have very powerful senses of smell and hearing, despite having no external ears.
- A snail's foot is covered with thousands of tiny hairs which help it move.
- Slugs can retract their bodies into their shells to protect themselves from predators.
- Snails breathe through a pair of 'lungs' located at the opening of their shells.
- Slugs can produce slime for defence, for movement and also to store water.
- Snails and slugs can regenerate lost body parts, such as antennae and eyes.
- Snails can live up to 10 years while slugs can live only 2 years.

- The biggest species of snail is the Giant African Land Snail, which can grow up to 30 cm in length.
- Slugs prefer dark and damp environments, while snails prefer dry and warm places.
- Snails and slugs are able to reproduce multiple times throughout the year.
- The common garden snail can travel up to 15 centimetres per hour.
- Many species of snail and slug are native to the tropics and subtropics.
- Slugs and snails can be found in cities, grasslands, forests, and even in deserts.

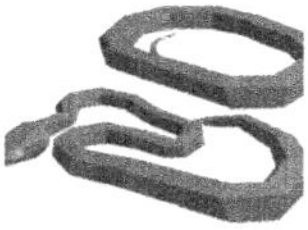

SNAKES

SNAKES ARE some of the most fascinating creatures in the world. They have adapted to almost every environment and evolved some amazing features to survive. They can move without legs and use their sense of smell to hunt. They can even recognize individual humans and are one of the few animal species on earth that can see in the infrared spectrum. Here are some amazing facts about snakes:

- Certain species of snakes can lay eggs, while others give birth to live young.
- The majority of snake species are non-venomous and harmless to humans.
- Snakes can climb trees and swim in water.
- Snakes can sense the vibration of their prey through the ground.
- Snakes shed their skin in one piece every few weeks.
- A king cobra can reach a length of 18 feet, making it the longest venomous snake in the world.
- A snake can eat a prey up to three times its own size.
- The longest living snake species can live up to 40 years.

- The boomslang is the only snake whose venom can cause internal bleeding.
- The garter snake is the most common species of snake in North America.
- The Brazilian rainbow boa has a prehensile tail, allowing it to use its tail to grab branches and other objects.
- The inland taipan is the most venomous snake in the world.
- The chicken snake is a species of snake known for its ability to mimic birds.
- The western hognose snake plays dead when threatened.
- Some species of snakes can change their color to blend in with their environment.

SPIDERS

SEE ALSO: TARANTULAS

SPIDERS ARE TRULY INCREDIBLE CREATURES, with some amazing facts about them that have been discovered by scientists. They come in a variety of shapes, sizes and colors and exhibit unique behaviors that make them fascinating to observe. Here are some amazing facts about spiders:

- Spiders have been around for about 300 million years, making them one of the oldest and most diverse group of animals on Earth.
- Spiders have up to 8 eyes, although not all species have the same number of eyes.
- Some spiders can jump up to 50 times their own body length.
- The average spider can produce up to 7 different types of silk, each made for a different purpose.
- Most spiders build webs to capture prey and some even use the vibrations of their webs to sense the presence of prey.
- Some spiders are capable of living underwater and can even breathe underwater.

- Many species of spiders have incredibly long lifespans, with some living up to 20-30 years in captivity.
- Some spiders are capable of changing colors, darkening or lightening their bodies for camouflage.
- Male spiders often have special courtship dances to attract a female.
- Spiders have special organs on their legs which allow them to sense vibrations in their environment.
- Spiders have no bones and instead depend on their exoskeleton made of tough chitin and proteins.
- Spiders can be found in almost every environment on every continent.
- Spiders can eat prey much larger than themselves and can even eat other spiders.
- Spiders can survive for months without food, relying on their stored body fat for sustenance.
- Spiders have special hairs on their bodies that allow them to sense air currents, making them incredible navigators.

SQUID

SQUIDS ARE a fascinating species of mollusk and they have some truly incredible abilities. They can change color in an instant to camouflage, shoot ink to confuse predators, move quickly and even control the light they reflect to stay hidden. Here are some amazing facts about squids:

- Squids have 3 hearts.
- Squids can grow to sizes of up to 43 feet in length.
- They can move around in any direction, even upside down.
- They have the ability to regenerate lost arms and tentacles.
- Squids communicate using special organs called chromatophores, which create color changes on their skin.
- All squids have two long tentacles, 8 shorter arms and a beak-like mouth.
- Their eyes are the most complex of any invertebrate.
- Squids have a powerful jet-propulsion system that can move them through the water at speeds of up to 25 mph.

- Squids have special organs called statocysts which help them sense the direction and speed of their motion.
- Squids use their tentacles to capture prey and to defend themselves.
- Squids have a special organ called a gladius, which is used to help them swim.
- They are able to release ink when threatened, creating a dark cloud to help them escape predators.
- There are more than 300 species of squids found in the world's oceans.
- Squids have very short lifespans, only living for up to two years.

SQUIRRELS

SQUIRRELS ARE INCREDIBLE RODENTS, with an impressive array of physical and behavioral adaptations that make them successful in a wide range of habitats. They are well known for their acrobatic skills for climbing, jumping, and balancing, with some species able to leap up to 6 metres from branch to branch. They also possess an impressive memory, allowing them to remember the location of their caches of food.

- Squirrels are found on every continent except Antarctica and Australia
- There are over 200 species of squirrels worldwide
- Squirrels use their powerful hind legs as a form of self-defense when startled
- Squirrels have incredibly strong jaws and teeth that continuously grow
- Squirrels are capable of swimming and have been seen using leaves to make a makeshift raft
- Their diet consists of a variety of nuts, seeds, fruits, and fungi

- Squirrels have an excellent sense of hearing and vision
- They are able to communicate with one another by a range of vocalizations and body language
- Some species of squirrels can glide for distances of up to 180 metres
- Squirrels prefer to live in family groups
- They use their tail for balance and as a form of protection from the elements
- Red squirrels are able to turn their back feet to adjust their position in the air while jumping
- Squirrels are solitary animals and mark their territory with scent glands to warn off other squirrels

STARFISH

STARFISH ARE an incredible and fascinating species of sea life. From their unique ability to regenerate lost limbs to their ability to absorb oxygen through their skin, they are an amazing example of ocean life. Here are some amazing facts about starfish:

- Starfish can have up to 50 arms.
- Starfish use their tube feet to move along the ocean floor.
- Starfish have a water vascular system which helps them move and digest food.
- Starfish can have a lifespan of up to 35 years.
- Starfish can emit a toxin to help protect themselves from predators.
- Starfish have the ability to change their color to match their surroundings.
- Starfish have an excellent sense of smell and taste.
- Some starfish are capable of eating their prey whole.
- Starfish have the ability to move their eyes around independently.
- Starfish have no brain or central nervous system.

- Starfish can be found in all the world's oceans, from shallow tidal pools to the deepest ocean depths.
- Some starfish are capable of complete asexual reproduction.
- Starfish can live in both salty and fresh water.

SWANS

SWANS ARE MAJESTIC, intelligent birds that have captivated humans throughout history. They are a source of wonder and admiration for their beautiful feathers, graceful movements, and affectionate behavior. Swans are known to mate for life, with some pairs staying together for many years. Here are some amazing facts about swans:

- Female swans are called pens, while males are known as cobs.
- Swans can live up to 30 years in the wild.
- Swans have a wingspan of up to 8 feet (2.4 m).
- Swans have over 25,000 feathers.
- Swans can fly at speeds of up to 60 mph (95 km/hr).
- Swans are excellent swimmers, able to cover long distances in the water.
- Swans are omnivorous, but their diet primarily consists of aquatic vegetation.
- Swans are social birds, often seen in large flocks.
- Swans can display aggressive behavior, particularly when protecting their nests.

- Swans use a variety of vocalizations, such as honks, whistles, and grunts.
- Swan eggs are generally white or cream-colored.
- Swans can lay up to 8 eggs per clutch.
- Swans are very protective of their young and will fiercely defend them.
- Swans can use their wings to 'clap' underwater to scare away potential predators.

TAPIRS

TAPIRS ARE REMARKABLE CREATURES, native to South and Central America, Southeast Asia and the Malay Peninsula. They are herbivores, and have unique features such as a short, prehensile snout. They are also highly intelligent. Amazing facts about tapirs:

- The tapir is the largest living land mammal in South and Central America.
- Their prehensile snout is used to grab food and manipulate objects.
- They are herbivores, and their diet consists of leaves, fruit, grasses, aquatic plants and bark.
- Tapirs can swim and remain submerged for up to 5 minutes.
- They are highly intelligent animals, capable of learning and remembering tasks.
- Tapirs are protected by law in many countries.
- Females give birth to a single calf after a gestation period of about 13 months.
- They have an excellent sense of hearing and smell.

- They are crepuscular, meaning they are most active at dawn and dusk.
- Tapirs have a lifespan of up to 30 years in the wild.
- They have a unique pattern of stripes and spots on their bodies.
- They have a special flap of skin on their stomachs, which helps them cool down in hot weather.
- Tapirs communicate through a variety of vocalizations.
- They are solitary animals, except during mating season.
- They inhabit tropical and subtropical rainforests, as well as grasslands, swamps, and rivers.

TARANTULAS

TARANTULAS ARE fascinating and incredible creatures. They are the biggest spiders in the world and have incredible physical abilities. They have specialized hairs that can detect vibrations, they can jump several feet in the air with the help of their back legs.

- Tarantulas can live up to 25 years.
- Tarantulas have fangs that can grow to be over 1 inch long.
- They can detect vibrations with specialized hairs located on their legs.
- They have a unique ability to shed their external skeletons, allowing them to grow bigger.
- They can jump several feet in the air with the help of their back legs.
- Tarantulas have eight eyes located on their carapace.
- They use their powerful claws to hold prey and defend themselves.
- They can move at speeds of up to 1.3 feet per second.

- They have the ability to release a silk line that can slow their descent when jumping from high places.
- Tarantulas can detect chemical signals such as pheromones.
- They have an acute sense of hearing and can respond to sound.
- They can survive without food or water for up to a year.
- They can produce a venom that can be deadly to small animals.
- They have hairs on their abdomen that can be used as defense against predators.
- Tarantulas are found on every continent except Antarctica.

TIGERS

TIGERS ARE one of the world's most amazing animals. They are the largest species of big cats, capable of reaching lengths of up to 3 meters. They also possess incredible strength and are capable of swimming across huge rivers.

- Tigers are the top predators in their ecosystems, eating deer, wild boar, and even elephants.
- The Sumatran tiger is the smallest of all tiger species, reaching only 2.2 meters in length.
- The Siberian tiger is the largest of all tiger species, weighing up to 300 kilograms.
- Tigers have a striped coat to help them blend into their environment and surprise their prey.
- Tigers' unique coats act as built-in camouflage, helping them to ambush their prey.
- Tigers can jump up to 5 meters in length, allowing them to quickly close in on their prey.
- Tigers have small ears relative to their body size, allowing them to better detect the sounds of their prey.

- Tigers have powerful jaws and sharp claws, allowing them to hunt and kill large prey.
- Tigers are solitary animals, usually hunting and living alone.
- Tigers have an exceptional sense of smell, allowing them to detect prey from up to 1.6 km away.
- Tigers use scent marks to mark their territories and communicate with other tigers.
- Tigers can reach speeds of up to 60 kilometers per hour while running.
- Tigers have an average lifespan of around 10 to 15 years in the wild.

TROPICAL BIRDS

SEE ALSO: HUMMINGBIRDS, PARROTS & MACAWS

TROPICAL BIRDS ARE INCREDIBLY diverse and colorful, and are home to some of the most striking and exotic species in the world. From toucans to macaws, hummingbirds to parrots, tropical birds provide a wealth of amazing facts and behavior.

- There are over 8,000 species of tropical birds.
- Many tropical birds can mimic human speech.
- Tropical birds rely heavily on their colorful plumage to attract mates.
- Some tropical birds can live up to 40 years in the wild.
- The largest tropical bird is the Andean Condor, which has a wingspan of up to 3m.
- The smallest tropical bird is the bee hummingbird, which measures just 5cm in length.
- The toucan has the largest beak-to-body ratio of any bird in the world.
- The quetzal is one of the most beautiful tropical birds, and is a symbol of freedom in many Central American countries.

- The aracari is the smallest member of the toucan family.
- The Victoria crowned pigeon is the largest species of pigeon in the world.
- The kea is a species of parrot that is found only in the mountains of New Zealand.
- The hoatzin is an unusual looking tropical bird found in the Amazon rainforest.
- The Nicobar pigeon is the only tropical bird to have a luminous green sheen.
- The Guianan cock-of-the-rock is a species of tropical bird that has a vibrant orange and red plumage.
- The lyrebird is renowned for its ability to mimic the calls of other bird species.

TURKEYS

TURKEYS ARE FASCINATING CREATURES, boasting many unique features. They can fly surprisingly fast, reaching speeds of up to 55 mph, and have an impressive vision that can even see in ultraviolet light. Their sense of hearing is also well-developed, with their hearing range extending beyond that of humans.

- Turkeys can fly at speeds up to 55 mph.
- They can see in ultraviolet light.
- Their hearing range extends beyond that of humans.
- Turkeys are adaptable to various climates and habitats.
- They can live up to 10 years in the wild.
- Turkeys can reproduce twice a year.
- Their heads can appear to change color when they are excited or alarmed.
- Male turkeys use their feathered beards to attract mates.
- The average turkey has 5,000 feathers.
- They can live up to five weeks without food or water.

- They are capable of recognizing over 100 different vocalizations.
- Wild turkeys can run up to 25 mph.
- Turkeys have a great sense of direction and can often find their way home from long distances.
- The longest recorded flight of a turkey is reportedly 300 yards.
- Turkeys spend most of the day foraging for food.

TURTLES AND TORTOISES

TURTLES AND TORTOISES are incredible creatures with an array of amazing characteristics. Some species can hold their breath for up to four hours and hibernate during the winter. Here is a list of 10 amazing facts about turtles and tortoises:

- Some species of turtles and tortoises can grow up to 2 meters in length.
- Turtles and tortoises have been around for over 200 million years.
- The leatherback turtle can swim up to speeds of 22 mph.
- Some species of turtles can survive in both salt water and fresh water.
- The hawksbill turtle can live up to 150 years or more.
- The Chinese three-striped box turtle is one of the rarest turtles in the world.
- The green turtle is the only species of sea turtle that is herbivorous.
- The Galapagos giant tortoise can weigh up to 400 kg.

- The gopher tortoise is the only tortoise found in the southeastern United States.
- The African spurred tortoise is the third largest species of tortoise in the world.
- The Australian pig-nosed turtle is the only freshwater turtle that has a snout like a pig!
- The red-eared slider turtle is one of the most popular pet turtles.
- The loggerhead turtle is the largest of all hard-shelled turtles.

VULTURES

VULTURES ARE INCREDIBLE BIRDS, with some amazing special features that help them to survive in challenging environments. They have incredibly acute vision! They have specialized wings which help them to soar for hours, and use up very little energy in doing so. Vultures also have acid-resistant stomachs which allow them to digest even the most decomposed carcasses. Here are some amazing facts about vultures:

- Vultures have bald heads to prevent them from getting blood and other fluids on their feathers while eating.
- Vultures can tell when a carcass is safe to eat by the smell of its gas emissions.
- Vultures can reach speeds of up to 55 miles an hour when gliding.
- Vultures have no vocal chords, and so they make no vocalizations.
- Vultures have impressive wingspans that can reach up to 9 feet.

- Vultures flap their wings very infrequently, allowing them to conserve energy and soar for hours.
- Vultures have special feathers which allow them to regulate their body temperature.
- Vultures can live for up to 30 years in the wild.
- Vultures have incredibly strong beaks which can break through tough hides.
- Vultures can consume up to 2.2 pounds of meat in a single sitting.
- Vultures can detect thermal currents which help them to spot prey from up to 30 miles away.
- Vultures will often gather in large groups to help locate and scavenge food.
- Vultures will regurgitate food if they feel threatened or feel they are in danger.

WALRUSES

WALRUSES ARE an impressive part of the animal kingdom, exhibiting a variety of unique traits and capabilities. They are the only living species of the Odobenidae family and are mostly found in the Arctic Ocean and its surrounding waters. Walruses have long tusks made of ivory, a thick layer of blubber which helps them keep warm, and a powerful sense of smell. Amazing facts about walruses:

- Walruses can grow up to 3.5 meters long and weigh up to 1.5 tons.
- They have two layers of fur, an outer layer of long guard hairs and an inner layer of short, dense underfur for insulation.
- Walruses can dive up to 60 metres below the surface and stay down for up to 30 minutes.
- They sleep in the water, using their tusks to anchor themselves to the seafloor.
- They are expert swimmers and can reach speeds of up to 25 km/hour.
- Walruses use their long tusks to break through thick sea ice in search of food.

- They use vocalisations and specialized movements to communicate with each other.
- Walruses mainly eat clams, which they suck out of the sea floor using their strong lips.
- They have a sense of hearing that's sensitive to low frequency sounds.
- Walruses are social animals and live in large herds of up to several thousand individuals.
- They have an advanced sense of smell and can detect their prey from up to a mile away.
- Walruses have whiskers on their faces and chins that help them to detect prey in murky water.
- They are capable of sleeping underwater for short periods of time.
- Walruses have been known to use rocks to help them open molluscs.
- They can live up to 40 years in the wild.

WHALES

WHALES ARE some of the most fascinating and captivating creatures on planet Earth. They are incredibly intelligent, acrobatic, and have extraordinary capabilities. Some of their amazing feats include swimming thousands of miles while changing their depth and direction, holding their breath for extended periods of time, and communicating with each other across long distances. Here are some truly amazing facts about whales:

- Whales are the largest animals on earth, with the biggest species reaching up to 30 meters in length.
- They can travel at speeds of up to 20 knots (37 km/h).
- They can dive up to 1,000 meters below sea level.
- Whales can produce a variety of sounds, including complex songs.
- They can live up to 90 years old.
- Whales are highly social animals and often gather in large groups.
- They use echolocation to "see" and navigate their environment.

- They have a huge appetite and can consume up to 1.5 tonnes of food a day.
- They can sense the Earth's magnetic field using magnetoreception.
- Whales are incredibly intelligent and can learn complex behaviors.
- Their blowholes allow them to breathe and store air for extended dives.
- Whales have a specialized layer of blubber to keep them warm in cold water.
- They use their tail fluke to propel themselves through the water.
- Whales have been observed rescuing other animals, including humans.

WOLVES

WOLVES ARE amazing animals that have a long history of being both feared and admired across the world. They have an impressive social structure and are renowned for their intelligence. Wolves are also incredibly adaptive and have a remarkable sense of hearing and smell. Here are some amazing facts about wolves:

- Wolves howl to communicate with each other, and the howl of a single wolf can be heard up to 10 miles away.
- Wolves have 42 teeth.
- Wolves are incredibly fast, and can run up to 35 miles per hour.
- Wolves are social animals and live in packs of 5 to 10 members.
- Wolves can jump up to 8 feet in the air.
- Wolves can swim up to 13 miles per hour.
- Wolves have a great sense of smell that is 100 times better than humans. It allows them to detect prey from 1.5 miles away.

- Wolves have an incredible sense of hearing that is 4 times better than humans.
- Wolves can see color, and have better vision in low light than humans.
- Wolves have a strong bond with their pack and typically mate for life.
- Wolves typically have one to seven pups per litter.
- Wolves are very protective of their territory, which can range from several hundred to several thousand square miles.
- Wolves have a vast range and can be found in parts of North America, Europe, Asia, and North Africa.
- Wolves are the largest member of the canine family and can weigh up to 175 pounds.

ZEBRAS

ZEBRAS ARE some of the most incredible animals on the planet. They are known for their distinctive black and white stripes, which are actually unique to each individual zebra and act as a type of camouflage when in a group. Zebras also have incredible physical strength and stamina, allowing them to outrun and outlast many of their predators. Here is a list of other amazing facts about zebras:

- Zebras are part of the Equidae family, which includes horses, donkeys and mules.
- Zebras are herbivores and predominantly feed on grass.
- Zebras live in groups of up to hundreds of individuals and form strong social bonds with one another.
- Zebras communicate with each other using a range of vocalizations, including snorts, barks, and brays.
- The average life expectancy of a zebra is 25-30 years.
- Zebras can reach speeds of up to 40 miles per hour when running.

- Zebras have excellent eyesight, allowing them to see predators from a great distance.
- Zebras are highly adaptable and can survive in a wide range of climates, from desert to grassland.
- Zebras are capable of swimming and will often cross rivers to reach new grazing grounds.
- Zebras have a four-chambered stomach, which allows them to digest tougher plant matter.
- Zebras have thick, leathery skin and a mane of fur to protect them from predators.
- The stripes of a zebra are thought to be an adaptation to help regulate its body temperature.
- Zebras have excellent hearing and can detect predators from far away.
- Zebras can recognize individual herd members and form lifelong bonds with them.
- Zebras are the only species of truly wild horse still in existence.

Printed in Great Britain
by Amazon

18577714R00133